My Life in the 50 States

Jodi C. Greve

Keep Exploring!

Jodi Greve

Published by Self Publish -N- 30 Days

Copyright 2019 Jodi Greve.

All rights reserved worldwide. No part of this book may be reproduced or transmitted in any form or by any means electronic or mechanical, including photocopying, recording or by any information storage and retrieval system without written permission from Jodi Greve.

Printed in the United States of America

ISBN: 978-1073752324 1. Memoir 2. Travel Jodi Greve

Michigan and Wisconsin images created by katemangostar via freepik.com

My Life in the 50 States

Disclaimer/Warning:
This book is intended for lecture and informative purposes only. The author or publisher does not guarantee that anyone reading this book will be successful in travel or life. The author and publisher shall have neither liability responsibility to anyone with respect to any loss or damage cause, or alleged to be caused, directly or indirectly by the information contained in this book.

TABLE OF CONTENTS

Acknowledgments V

Introduction 1

Alabama 3

Alaska 7

Arizona 11

Arkansas 15

California 19

Colorado 25

Connecticut 27

Delaware 29

Florida 31

Georgia 35

Hawaii 39

Idaho 45

Illinois 47

Indiana 51

Iowa 55

Kansas 59

Kentucky 63

Louisiana 65

Maine 67

Maryland 71

Massachusetts 75

Michigan 77

Minnesota 81

Mississippi 85

Missouri 87

Montana 91

Nevada 93

Nebraska 99

New Hampshire 103

New Jersey 105

New Mexico	109	Tennessee	153
New York	111	Texas	159
North Carolina	119	Utah	163
North Dakota	125	Vermont	165
Ohio	129	Virginia	169
Oklahoma	131	Washington	171
Oregon	133	West Virginia	177
Pennsylvania	139	Wisconsin	183
Rhode Island	143	Wyoming	187
South Carolina	145	Bonus Info	189
South Dakota	149	50 States Gallery	193

ACKNOWLEDGMENTS

Never in my wildest dreams did I ever think I would write a book. I am a numbers gal. Math was, and still is, my favorite subject. Writing was always difficult for me because I felt like I never had an extensive enough vocabulary to be able to put my vivid imagination into words. When reading a book, I would always wonder how authors did it. How did they know how to make a paragraph flow to the next? When it came down to me writing this, it was easy. I knew the outcome of every story. I didn't have to create anything. It was simple because I lived it all.

I want to thank everyone for their continued support through everything. My friends may always be teasing me about my life on the go, but I feel honored when they introduce me as their friend, "Jodi, the Gypsy" and "She's the one I've told you about who travels everywhere." My family may not see me as often as we'd like, but every time I go home, we get to sit and talk about my latest adventures and discuss the next possible one.

None of this would have been possible without my parents. I am not sure how exactly they taught me to be adventurous, see the world or be independent, but I am thankful they did. I was

ACKNOWLEDGMENTS

very blessed to have been adopted by John and Diane Greve. People often ask me about my "real parents." My answer is simple. They live in a small south Texas town. They are my real parents. They are all I have ever known or wanted to know. They raised me and gave me a life that is, I'm fairly certain, far better than the one I would have had. Our life wasn't always easy growing up, but that is ok. They taught me how to appreciate the little things and never take the big things for granted. They taught me to give, even if it is only your time you have to give. They taught me to love everyone no matter what. Most importantly, they taught me to be thankful.

So Mom and Dad, thank you.

INTRODUCTION

I HAVE ALWAYS LOVED TO travel, meet new people and see new things. I am not sure exactly where I got this urge from, but I never want to be still or idle. Some time ago, I had a conversation with a woman, and the topic of conversation gave me my new bucket list item. We were on a Southwest flight and began discussing why we were traveling. At the time, I was traveling for recruiting purposes, as I was a collegiate women's basketball coach. She was traveling on business as well. We began to talk about all the states that we each had visited. If you've ever been on a Southwest flight, you know their napkins have a map of the United States on the back. We both started counting the states and I realized there were only 12 states that I had not visited: Alaska, Connecticut, Delaware, Maine, Michigan, Minnesota, New Hampshire, North and South Dakota, Rhode Island, Vermont and Wisconsin.

Basketball took me to the majority of the states I had visited. A few others were due to my dad changing jobs when I was younger. Right then I realized I wanted to hit all 50 states by the time I was 50. I had no idea how I would get to New England, let alone the

INTRODUCTION

Dakotas. I mean, who goes to the Dakotas if they don't know anyone there? I thought about how I could make this happen. I even discussed it with a dear friend of mine every time I saw him out on the road recruiting. We both wanted to do a road trip through New England. It was small enough that we could make a trip in a week and easily hit six states. Coaching college basketball, it was important that we were able to accomplish it in a week because coaches do not get much time off. Knocking off the others was going to be quite the challenge, but I had some years before I was 50. However, 50 before 50 quickly became 50 before 40 and then after a road trip through four of my last five states, I wanted to get that last state out of the way before the end of 2017.

I had quite an experience in every single state. In some, I reflected on life and/or experienced life, and some were places where a girl was able to just have fun! This book is going to allow you to travel with me through each state and give you a brief peek into the unique experiences that each state presented.

ALABAMA
May 1997

I was finishing my freshman year of college and was supposed to drive from Odessa, Texas, to Rural Hall, North Carolina, to visit my parents for the summer. I was paranoid about the possibility of my parents finding out about my tattoo that I got seven months prior (one that I also hid through a surgery and the Christmas holidays). My suitemate, Natalie, who was also my teammate, was from Montgomery, Alabama, and she didn't know how she was going to get home.

I told her if she would help me drive and chip in on some money for gas, we could hit the road for an epic college road trip. So, she being a black woman from Montgomery who had never been around white people daily until she got to college nine months before, jumped in the car with me. She warned me that when we arrived people would come over, watch and wonder why there was a white woman in their neighborhood and why on earth was she staying at her house. I shook it off and didn't believe her. That type of stuff only happens in the movies. Not in real life any more. Boy, was I wrong.

We headed southeast, and our first stop was in my hometown

ALABAMA

of Kenedy, Texas, at my grandmother's house for the first night. Natalie absolutely adored my grandmother and the feeling was mutual. For years after, both would ask about how the other was doing. Our next stop was in Lake Charles, Louisiana, to eat lunch with my aunt. We were hoping to make it all the way to Montgomery that day, but Mother Nature had other plans as we were driving through Mississippi. This is where I had the most eye-opening experience of my life up until that time. (You can read about this experience under Mississippi.)

We left before dawn the next day to continue. When we got close, Natalie reminded me of the reaction people would have. I still didn't believe her. When we turned on her street there were a couple of older men sitting on the porch and I heard one of them yell, "Natalie, why you have that white bitch with you?" I turned beet red and was scared as hell. Nat looked at me and said, "I told you. But don't worry. You are with me and you will be ok."

As we drove down the street, which seemed like a very long mile, people started coming out of their homes and just stared. I could tell that she was well-liked in her neighborhood as everyone on their porches were yelling things like, "Welcome home, Natalie!" or "Glad to have you home, Nat!"

Once we got to her house and parked, two kids—a skinny young boy and a beautiful chunky girl—from across the street ran across to greet Natalie. The boy helped us unload our car and the shy young girl just stood against the garage remaining quiet and watching us. Once we could get everything inside, I noticed the girl couldn't stop staring at me and I had no idea why.

"You know why she keeps staring at you?" Natalie asked.

"Not a clue," I said.

MY LIFE IN THE 50 STATES

"She's never been this close to a white person before," she replied.

I couldn't believe what she was telling me. This is not real life. It can't be real life. How in the world was this true? Natalie went on to explain that Montgomery was still the Old South. Railroad tracks separated the whites and the blacks. I was flabbergasted. I thought segregation had ended in the 60s. I had no idea that it was still relevant in 1997. Her mom worked at a country club where it was a predominately all-white membership and much of the staff were black. It was so hard for my mind to process this.

More people started to ring the doorbell and welcome Natalie home. She said some were genuine in their welcoming, but most were just nosy as to whom she brought home and why. While she was in the living room welcoming people, I stayed in the back with the kids and tried to make small conversation about school with the little girl, but she was hesitant to answer any questions. She couldn't stop staring at me though. I didn't mind because she stared at me with the cutest smile.

As all the visitors came in and out of the house, I tried to be as polite and respectful as one should be, and I tried to engage in as much conversation as possible, partly because it is the right thing to do, but mainly because I didn't want them to think I was a "bitch" like the man down the street had called me without even knowing who I was. It bothered me. It really bothered me that someone would think of me one way without even knowing who I was.

Throughout the few days I was there, Natalie took me around to different places and I got to meet different people. One evening we stopped at a random gas station/restaurant. We walk in and see some older men sitting at a table. Natalie begins to chat it up

ALABAMA

with the men. I try to engage in conversation. One of the men was very aggressive in asking me all kinds of questions, but they were all about me, so I was not having a problem answering. The gentleman seemed shocked that I wasn't getting defensive or scared. Before we walked out, he told Natalie, "Your friend is all right with us." I thought it was cool that one of the guys gave me their approval, although I'm not sure why.

Once we got in the car, Natalie asked if I knew who that was. I shook my head and as she laughed, she reminded me of the guy who called me a bitch when we first rolled into the neighborhood. "It was him."

ALASKA
August 2015

My first summer out of coaching. I couldn't believe I was out of coaching. I also couldn't believe I was going on a cruise to Alaska. One, I wasn't so fond of the idea of a cruise and the possibility of getting seasick. Two, even though it was summer, I wasn't thrilled about how cold it would be there. I despise being cold and I get motion sickness just from riding down the street.

Nonetheless, I was meeting my parents, my brother, Scott, sister-in-law, Jessica, my oldest nephew, Aiden, and her sister, Kat, in Seattle to head out on a weeklong cruise to Alaska. We made stops in Juneau, Ketchikan, Skagway, the Tracy Arm Fjord and Victoria, British Columbia.

Our first stop was in Juneau. We had signed up to go whale watching. The unique thing about this excursion is that you are not guaranteed to see any whales. All you can do is hope and pray that your boat is in the right spot at the right time. As we set off on the four-hour ride, one of the guides started giving us information about the area—what type of marine life was in the area and their tendencies of living and migration.

ALASKA

After the short talk, I left to walk around. I wanted to make sure I saw whatever there was to be seen. I did not want to miss any opportunity to see a whale. We didn't have to wait long. I heard a bit of commotion out on the deck, so I ran outside and started recording on my phone. I didn't know what I might capture, if anything at all. All of a sudden, a young male humpback whale emerged from the water, breaching high above the surface. He was very playful and having fun. It was so surreal to see something in nature that you had only seen on the National Geographic or Discovery Channel. And five seconds later he did it again.

I know these animals are huge. But to see them rise out of the water and then come crashing down put it into perspective. The guide announced over the loud speaker that it was rare that a young calf would breach the water that much that time of year. I felt the luck that day. Although we saw more pods of whales, we didn't see any more breach the water.

Our stop in Ketchikan allowed us to go on one of the crab boats that was once on the Discovery Channel show *Deadliest Catch*. After encountering a 50-foot wave, the captain/owner of the Aleutian Ballad decided to retire it from expeditions during crab fishing seasons. It now takes visitors around the bay to educate people on how crab fishing works, as well as to watch for the many bald eagles that inhabit that part of the state. The boat crew presets the crab pots and sometimes when they pull them up, other creatures are found in the pots. The group on the tour before us found a large octopus in the crab pot.

The fisherman's plan was to "teach the octopus a lesson" by putting him in a dark garbage-can-like container in the water. On our trip, they reeled it in, showed us the monstrous creature and

MY LIFE IN THE 50 STATES

then let him go back into the water. It served two purposes. One, to show us curious tourists a little more of the wild and two, to hopefully deter the octopus from getting back into the pot.

After another night at sea, we made port in Skagway. Once we arrived, we took a walk around the town before boarding a train for a 20-mile ride through the Alaskan mountains. We saw massive mountains that were above fields of green trees and blooming flowers.

The train route took us on the same route that the gold miners of the 1800s took by mules and foot. The wooden bridges were just as rickety as they should have been for being almost 150 years old. It was scary and I was nervous about the train crossing the bridge, but felt like we were riding back in time. This train ride took us across the Canadian border before we switched directions and headed back towards Skagway. The mountainous scenery along this train ride was unlike any I have ever experienced in the lower 48 states.

Alaska was one of the many states I originally didn't want to visit, because I only thought of one thing when anyone mentioned Alaska—cold. After visiting during the summer when it was unseasonably warm, I cannot wait to go back. It is so hard to describe the size of the mountains. I've been to the Rockies in Colorado. I've been to the Appalachian Mountains in North Carolina. Those are rolling hills compared to what is in Alaska. Besides the bald eagles and humpback whales, I didn't get to see much wildlife, so this would be on my list of things to see when I go back—in the summer, of course.

ARIZONA
December 1993

IT WAS THE MIDDLE OF my sophomore year. I was furious with my parents. I was moving from Del Rio, Texas, to Sierra Vista, Arizona. My brother had graduated high school the previous May, so it was just me in the house. I played basketball all through high school, so this also meant I was moving in the middle of the season to a new team.

My parents knew before my sophomore year started that we would be moving, and so did my coaches. That meant I had zero chance to make varsity as a sophomore. The coaches weren't about to put someone on the team who wouldn't be there the entire year. This also meant I was going to have to hope that the new basketball coach would let me join their team midseason.

We drove to Arizona just before Christmas of 1993. We pulled up to a rental house that my dad had found until we could find a house to buy. It was considerably smaller than our house in Del Rio and just full of boxes. I remember the first night we spent there. I didn't have a television in my room but had a radio alarm clock. I fell asleep listening to Toni Braxton's song, "Breathe Again." To this day, any time I hear that song, I remember the

ARIZONA

cold, alone, mad and scared feelings I felt that first night in Arizona.

My paternal grandfather, Chuck, who was 83 at the time, and his girlfriend, Jane, who was 79, were in town visiting. They were both very petite people and the cutest older couple you had ever seen. My grandmother, Audine, had died due to Alzheimer's two years prior. Soon after she had passed, my grandfather moved into the Las Palmas Assisted Living Facility where he met Jane. The two fell in love and would later be the first couple to marry at the facility (on her 80th birthday).

They were our first, and only, visitors to Arizona. Our Christmas was spent around a bunch of boxes. We didn't have any decorations or presents. As a teenager, I didn't understand why, after moving me a thousand miles away, they couldn't even get me any presents! The fact that we had a home, Dad had a job and we had each other should have been enough. I was a brat about it and, of course, acted up. Little did I know that in the next few days, Mom and Dad were taking me shopping for new bedroom furniture, which I still have in one of my bedrooms in my house.

My first day of school was also the first day for about 150 other students. It was a military town, the home of Fort Huachuca, so there were many new families due to parents' transfer orders. The process moved like clockwork. They called about 10–15 students at a time to meet with the counselors to set up their schedule. The rest of us waited in an auditorium. This was way before cell phones, so there was no fun way to pass the time. Eventually, it was my turn and I went to do my schedule.

When we finished, it was only 11:00 a.m. and the counselor asked if I wanted to go ahead and go to my next class. I looked

MY LIFE IN THE 50 STATES

at my mom, hoping she would say I could just go home, and we could start fresh in the morning. Unfortunately, my mom didn't see it the same way. She quickly said, "Yes," told me goodbye and that she would pick me up at 2:15 p.m. when school let out. I went on to class and cried at my desk when I sat down.

The only thing that kept me going was that later I was going to talk to the basketball coach. They did basketball a little different in Arizona and didn't have a varsity athletic period like we had in Texas. You also had to pay to play any varsity sport. It cost $25 for your first sport. It didn't matter, because I would have paid $100 if I had to. Basketball was my outlet. The junior varsity coach didn't work on campus, so I had to wait and meet her at practice, which wasn't until 5:00 p.m. because of her job. I was nervous, but confident I would make the team.

That day I talked with the coach and she told me to come back when I had a physical and I could go through a couple of practices, just to make sure I was talented enough for the JV team. Normally, they didn't allow move-ins to be added to the team midseason. The thought of not being able to play basketball after moving two states away only made me angrier at my dad for taking this job.

The next day, I was ready to go for practice 30 minutes early. I did not want to make a bad impression on the new coach. I HAD to make the team. As we were going through drills, I was trying to do everything perfect. I was talking, clapping and doing all the little things every other coach I had before said was important. I wasn't worried so much about my talent. I knew I was good enough. I believed I was good enough for the varsity team. I was worried about their willingness to add me midseason.

My adrenaline had me going like Wonder Woman, and it's good because the only exercise I had been able to get in a month

13

ARIZONA

were some ball handling drills outside of my house and running in the neighborhood. I felt like practice was as flawless as it could have been for my lack of conditioning.

Originally the coach told me I would have to go through several practices, so when she called me over after the first practice, I was scared she was going to deliver some bad news. She wasted no time and said she would love to add me to her team. I wanted to jump up and down, but tried to keep it cool with a cheesy ear-to-ear grin and saying *thank you* about 100 times.

Basketball is the one thing that helped me get through those 10 months that I lived in Arizona. Yes, I said 10 months. September of my junior year my dad received another job offer that he couldn't refuse. So, on Halloween of that year, Mom and I moved back to my hometown of Kenedy, Texas, to help my grandparents on the ranch and Dad moved to Rural Hall, North Carolina.

ARKANSAS
October 1998

TWO SUMMERS PRIOR, I had the opportunity to meet Coach Nolan Richardson in North Carolina (this is a great story and I will tell it later in North Carolina). Because of this, I became a trainer for the men's basketball team at the University of Arkansas. Honestly, before this was even an option, I couldn't ever remember if Arkansas or Missouri was north of Louisiana.

Being from Texas, there were so many options of college teams to cheer for. Texas, Texas A&M and Texas Tech, just to name a few. I have many Aggies in my family and my dad attended Texas for a few years. If you know anything of the old Southwest Conference, you know Arkansas was a huge rival to Texas.

Unfortunately, I haven't been able to talk too much trash the last five years when it comes to football. Especially to all the Aggies I have in my family. I didn't realize what I was getting into when I decided to attend Arkansas AND work for a sports team. The Razorbacks are IT in the state. They are the state's professional team. (There is no true professional team.) They are the only Power 5 Division I school in the state. Yes, UA Little Rock and Arkansas State are Division I, but not the same level.

ARKANSAS

I was planning to major in athletic training and becoming a trainer for a high school. That's what I came to Arkansas to do. About two months in, I changed my mind. As an athletic trainer, your main job is the prevention and care of athletic injuries. The trainer works to rehabilitate the athletes when they are injured and get them back on the court as soon as possible. I felt like this was a great opportunity for me to be able to stay in athletics. I tore my anterior cruciate ligament my freshman year in college and faced reality. I wasn't going to play after junior college, and I wanted to still be around the sport. I spent a lot of time in the training room and was very comfortable there. Athletic training seemed like the best opportunity for me to do that.

Starting out as a trainer for the men's team, I wasn't allowed to do as much hands-on treatment as I would have liked, but understood this was a part of any internship. The one thing I did do was watch Coach Richardson coach with passion and fire. He would pace the sidelines, occasionally breaking out in a slight run as the boys played full court. He got everything he could possibly get out of those guys. And he loved every minute of it. I realized that I had that same passion. I realized I wanted to do that too.

Over the course of those first couple of months, I became close with one of the then assistants, Mike Anderson. I decided to confide in him that I wanted to coach basketball in college, but had no idea how to get started.

I only played one year of junior college basketball and I was working with a men's team. He is the one who gave me the advice to work different basketball camps during the summertime, travel to as many schools that would take me as a summer camp coach and network. I didn't use this advice the first summer he gave it to me; however, I did use it the following summer. Coach

16

MY LIFE IN THE 50 STATES

A, as he is known, became a mentor to me on how to become a coach. Not only how to be on the floor, but also how to act off the floor. He and his wife, Marcheita, have become my second parents, as I call them, and my bonus sisters Darcheita, Yvonne, Suney (their niece) and brother Michael, Jr. Twenty years later, they still haven't been able to get rid of me.

My time in Arkansas was made great because of that family and Nolan Richardson. It was so great that when I decided to take a time-out after 14 years of coaching collegiate women's basketball, I moved back to Fayetteville where Coach A was the head basketball coach for the Razorbacks. Arkansas not only gave me the start to my coaching career, but a bonus family as well.

CALIFORNIA
May 2008

I WAS FINISHING UP MY first year of coaching at San Jose State. During the three years I lived in California, I truly thought I was living in a movie. The experience I will share here was definitely one of them.

In October of 2006, I was in Birmingham, Alabama, for Darcheita's wedding. She is like a sister to me, and she also happens to be the oldest daughter to Coach A and Marcheita. We went out the night before the wedding and found ourselves in a hole-in-the-wall club that had maybe fifty people there that night. We had a blast, but decided to call it a night around midnight since she was getting married the next day. I was ready to get out of my shoes and, as always, walked like a speed demon toward the door.

When I realized I was by myself, I turned around to see Darcheita at an empty bar, waiting on something (or someone). I walked over to see what was happening and she said she saw Charles Barkley around the corner. Since he was an SEC alum (he played college basketball at Auburn), she was going to see if she could just say hi.

CALIFORNIA

He came to the bar and we introduced ourselves. He asked where we were from and what we were in town for. He asked both of us what we did for a living and when I told him I coached college basketball, he seemed a little surprised. I was coaching at Tyler Junior College at the time, which is about two and a half hours from Dallas. He mentioned he might be going to Dallas at some point during the season, so I gave him a business card. I had zero belief that I would ever hear from him. When I got back to Texas, I couldn't help but brag that I met Charles Barkley. Some of my coworkers did not seem to believe me.

One January night, I received a phone call from an unrecognizable number. I answered, and the person on the other end said he was Chuck.

I said, "Chuck who? I only know one Chuck and I work with him."

He replied, "No, Charles Barkley. Don't you remember meeting me?"

HOLY SCHNIKES!!! Charles Barkley called me! We chatted a bit and he said he was going to be in Dallas in a few weeks. Unfortunately, I had a game the same time he was going to be in Dallas. I was disappointed, but he said he would stay in touch. Over the next couple of years, we would text during basketball season to catch up with one another.

Fast forward to the spring of 2008 when the San Antonio Spurs were playing the Los Angeles Lakers in the Western Conference Finals. Sometimes the TNT crew, which he worked for, travels to the conference finals games, so I threw it out there to him to see if he would be in Los Angeles. He was and asked if I wanted to come down. Because I knew I would not be able to get off of work, I was not able to go to the game, but decided to make the quick

MY LIFE IN THE 50 STATES

trip down to LA for the night. Why not? There was nothing in San Jose for me to do, so I figured I might as well hit the road! Road tripping was something I did quite often, so the five-hour drive down south was easy for me.

When I got to my hotel, I was still a little nervous about whether I should be there and go out. I mean, this is one of the best NBA players of all time. And I am, well, I am not. I went to dinner and came back to the hotel waiting to see what the plans were for the evening. Not too long after the game, I got a phone call and it was Charles. He is exactly as you see on television, straight-forward and to-the-point.

"Well are you going to meet us out or not?" he said.

I laughed to myself and said, "Yes, just tell me where to meet you."

He gave me the name of the club and told me he would leave my name at the front, so security would let me in right away. I had no idea where exactly I was going, but when I saw the sign that I was now in Beverly Hills in my Honda Civic, I felt a bit out of place. I remember pulling all the way up to the front of the valet so people right at the door wouldn't see me get out of my car.

Walking up to the door, I had more fear and anxiety run over me as I wondered if this was a prank and he really did not leave my name at the front. I was so nervous I was going to look like a crazy person telling the bouncer that Charles Barkley was supposed to have left my name at the front door.

To my surprise, when I walked up to the stand, I barely said my first name and the burly Italian man said, "Oh yes, we were expecting you. I will take you to the table right away." This was the first time in my life I ever felt like a VIP of any sort, as he led me to a VIP table upstairs.

21

CALIFORNIA

The anxiety settled a little, but I was still uneasy until we turned the corner at the top of the stairs, and I saw him standing in the corner at their table. I felt better when he recognized me and met me half way.

He gave me a big hug and said, "So glad you came! I want to introduce you to one of my friends." As we walked over to the table, I was looking down trying to make sure I didn't trip over anything, so I didn't see who he was talking about. "Jodi, this is my good friend, Reggie." I looked up and Reggie Miller has his hand extended out to shake mine. I about lost my breath. Two of the best NBA players, EVER, were right next to me. I was in complete awe. Of course, I know they are just people, but for a basketball coach, former player and fan like myself, this was pretty damn awesome.

The rest of the night was a lot of fun, hanging out with them and a few of the others who worked on the show behind the cameras, until it came time to leave. I had gone to the restroom and came out to a great deal of chaos. I have no idea what happened, but Charles met me and said we had to leave immediately. We were going out the back stairs and I was worried about my car. He had already told the valet to bring it around. I asked what happened and he said it was just time to get out of there.

As the valet brought my car around, Reggie had already left and I gave Charles (it's ok that I call them by their first names, right?) a hug and said thank you about 10 times. He thanked me for joining them, hopped in his black SUV and we went our separate ways. I was so giddy that night in my hotel I could barely sleep. I had just hung out with probably the best shooter and one of the best rebounders ever in the NBA.

The next day my ride home was almost as spectacular. I drove

MY LIFE IN THE 50 STATES

down Interstate 5, which cuts through the middle of the state. It isn't the most scenic drive and if the wind is blowing the wrong way, you will smell the dairy farms long before you see them. I decided I was going to drive home on the PCH (Pacific Coast Highway). I had heard about how beautiful this drive was and had seen it in several movies. To take that route was not going to take additional time, so I decided I should do it because I had no idea if that opportunity would ever present itself again.

As I began the drive, I was immediately thankful. The highway runs parallel to the coast, giving me a scenic route the entire way. I was able to see the Hearst Castle (google this and Patty Hearst, fascinating story), thousands of seals sleeping on the beach and one of the most beautiful sunsets I have ever seen.

The only difference between a movie and my real life at that moment was I didn't have a convertible to drive along the PCH with my hair blowing in the wind.

COLORADO
November 2008

I WAS COACHING AT San Jose State at the time. We had just finished playing a game at Northern Colorado (and lost... bad). The previous game, we had played great against Oregon and lost only by one. Going into the Northern Colorado game, we had high expectations for our team and those expectations were NOT met. We played one of the worst games, shooting a dismal 37% from the field, got outrebounded 41–30 and had 17 turnovers. That will not win you any games on the road.

We had to drive an hour to Denver that night in order to catch an early flight back to the Bay the next morning. The head coach I worked for at the time wanted to meet with the staff in the hotel room after the game to talk about the loss. We had just gotten beat by a good team, but we should not have been beaten 101–63. We all knew this.

I was exhausted not only from the game, but also from the travel I had prior to the game. As the recruiting coordinator, I spent a great deal of my time on the road recruiting. Prior to the Northern Colorado game, I was in Southern California watching games and flew in late the night before our game to meet the team.

COLORADO

Once we got settled at the hotel, we met in Brett's room. He was one of the other assistant coaches on the staff. Mistake #1—I chose the empty bed to sit on. Our head coach was sitting in one of the chairs, Brett was on his bed, and our other assistant, Megan, and the director of basketball operations, Angela, chose to sit on the floor.

I can't even tell you what we talked about that night, because, mistake #2—I decided to lay down. I am not sure what in my mind at that time could have possibly made me think I would stay awake at midnight on a Marriott hotel bed. I did, however, keep waking up when I heard an alarm on someone's phone go off.

Around 1:00 a.m. we finally left, and I asked about the alarm that that kept going off. Turns out, it was an alarm to remind Megan to take her medicine. That night was rough, and so was the rest of our season.

CONNECTICUT
August 2016

I WAS FINISHING A 10-day road trip through New England. I discovered a lot on this road trip. Not just about the country, but about myself. I will save that for Maine. The beginning of my road trip began with a seminar in Hartford, Connecticut. The end of it was a game between the Connecticut Sun and Minnesota Lynx.

One of the assistants at the time was Nikki Collen, who is now the head coach of the Atlanta Dream. I knew her from her time coaching at the University of Arkansas. I reached out on a whim to see if I could get a ticket for the game. She obliged, and I was going to get to see only my third WNBA game.

I was driving from Cape Cod, Massachusetts, so I checked and double-checked the time of the game several times that day to make sure I allowed myself enough time. The plan was to stop in Rhode Island for lunch, do a little shopping and then head to Connecticut for the game. (My time in Rhode Island was very entertaining. If you'd like, skip to that state now to read about it, and come right back.)

The app on my phone told me the game was at 6:30 p.m. I

CONNECTICUT

have this weird fear/nervousness of going somewhere I have never been before and ending up in the wrong place. Pretty interesting for someone who loves to travel, right?

Picking up from the Rhode Island story, I was late arriving to the Mohegan Sun, the casino where the Sun plays. As I arrived to the casino, there were no signs for the arena; at least not at the entrance I was coming in. I went to the first set of elevators and just guessed from there. I felt better parking and then walking, even if I had to walk a long way.

Fortunately for me, the elevator had several places within the casino listed on the door and I found the arena fairly quickly. As I hustled off the elevator, I checked my watch and it was 6:25 p.m. I was disappointed because I wanted to be able to watch warm-ups.

I approached the will-call window and had another slight anxiety moment. Any time I go to a game and people leave me tickets, I am worried that they forgot, or the right person didn't get the message or because my name is spelled wrong the ticket office won't give me the tickets. People spell my name wrong all the time. Yes, that's just how my mind can work sometimes.

As the worker checked for my tickets, I noticed that there was hardly anyone in the arena from what I could tell. I finally got my ticket and looked at it to see where my seat was located. When I did, I noticed the time on the ticket ... 7:30 p.m. I checked my phone to see what time it was, 6:30 p.m.

I checked my app again for the time and it said 6:30 p.m. That is when I realized that all the times of games on this particular app show the game times in my home time zone, which is Central Time Zone. Hey, at least I got to see them warm up like I wanted to.

DELAWARE
February 2017

I was in Philadelphia visiting Megan (my former coworker from San Jose State) and Joe (her then fiancé, now husband) for a few days. I had flown up there for a seminar in New Jersey and wanted to knock Delaware off my list. How exactly I was going to do this was to be determined. It was Super Bowl Sunday and Megan had to work. Joe offered to take me there (it is only about 30 minutes from their house), and we could go to one of their favorite stores for necessities for the Super Bowl. Yes, it was a liquor store.

This trip wasn't going to be very exciting. It was more a matter of going just for the sake of me saying I was going. We went to their favorite store and I tried to find a key chain of any kind to prove I had been to Delaware. When I didn't find one, I looked in the gas station and drug store next to it. No luck.

Joe said the University of Delaware was only another 10–15 minutes away if we wanted to go there. Of course, I wasn't about to say no. He took me through a quick campus drive, and we were able to find the bookstore. Since the bookstore was located on a narrow street with very little parking, Joe pulled up to the door so

DELAWARE

I could quickly hop out of the car. He drove around the block a few times which allowed me enough time to search out a University of Delaware key chain.

It took about three hours from the time we left the house to go to breakfast, drive to Delaware, go to the store, drive through UD's campus and get back to their house. Being from Texas, it still amazes me I could do all of that and be back home in three hours.

FLORIDA
May 2007

I had just accepted my first Division I assistant coaching job at San Jose State. Since this was the first time Brett and I were coaching on the Division I level, our head coach thought it would be a good idea to send us to a conference where they covered a great deal of compliance rules for Division I. It would be the first time I had ever been to Miami and it was going to be quite the memorable visit.

My head coach and Brett had just moved to California from Boca Raton, Florida, so they flew into Ft. Lauderdale to be able to visit a few friends and family. They would later drive over for the conference. I flew to Miami by myself the day before the conference was to begin.

I got checked in at the hotel and decided to head to the bar to grab some dinner. At the time, my go-to drink was Bacardi and Diet Coke. I ordered one of those and some dinner. I noticed that people started coming in as if they had all arrived on the same flight. The bar in the restaurant quickly got packed.

I made small talk with the bartender as well as the gentleman sitting next to me. Eventually it got so packed in there that

FLORIDA

people were coming up on my side trying to order drinks. I started talking to another gentleman who had squeezed his way in at the crowded bar to order a drink.

After finishing my drink and two glasses of water, I really had to go to the bathroom, but I had just ordered another drink. I asked the bartender if I could still save my seat and my drink and the gentleman assured me he would watch it and make sure no one would take it. (**NEVER, EVER, EVER, EVER DO THIS.**)

I went to the restroom and came back where my seat had been saved, as well as the drink I had just ordered. I continued to drink it, snack on some peanuts and talk to the people around me, just trying to meet more people. Within about 20 minutes I started to feel horrible. I can't describe the feeling, but I knew I wasn't feeling myself.

I barely remember leaving the bar and asking someone for directions to the restroom, but then got on the elevator instead to head to my room. I do NOT remember how I got to my room or even how I got in. The next thing I do remember is throwing up violently in the bathroom. I had never been sick like that in my life and to this day, I still haven't been that sick.

I woke up the next morning and couldn't remember where I was for the first 10 seconds I was awake. I couldn't find my phone. I called down to the front desk and someone from the bar had turned it in when they realized I wasn't coming back. I was very appreciative of that stranger. I was also very thankful that no one came with me back to my room, because well, I am just very thankful.

Obviously, I was very hung over, and I had already slept through the first meeting I was supposed to attend. I was struggling to try and get myself ready for the next meeting and was scared to face

MY LIFE IN THE 50 STATES

my head coach. I could only imagine what she was going to say. And whatever she was going to say, I deserved. I shouldn't have left my drink at the bar, under any circumstance. I shouldn't have put myself in that situation. I have no proof that I was drugged that night, but I am 98% sure I was. I don't know who it was that put something in my drink, but I have my own theory.

When I think about it, I am just thankful that getting sick was the worst thing that happened to me, because it could have been much worse. So much worse.

GEORGIA
August 1996

GEORGIA IS A BEAUTIFUL STATE. The first time I went to Georgia was one of the best presents ever. I graduated high school in 1996. At the time, my dad was working for Sara Lee in Winston Salem, North Carolina. Sara Lee had a knit product division, which many people were not aware of. The company made all of the underwear and apparel for Hanes, Hanes Her Way, Champion, and several others. Hanes was a huge sponsor for the 1996 Atlanta Olympics.

My graduation present was going to the Olympics. THE OLYMPICS!!!! As a child I always watched and dreamed of participating in them. This was the next best thing.

The employees of Sara Lee were given the opportunity to buy tickets earlier than the public. When my dad got the information to buy the tickets, he gave me a dollar amount to spend and told me to pick out what events we were going to see. I immediately knew I wanted to see basketball and track and field.

During the time that my dad was living in Winston Salem, my mom and I were living in Texas with my grandparents. She and I flew from Texas to Atlanta, where my dad had already arrived

GEORGIA

and picked us up from the airport. My excitement for attending the Olympics was hard to contain. I mean it's the OLYMPICS—the world's best athletes all in one spot!! I don't remember much about where we stayed, but knowing my dad it was a very inexpensive hotel. Clearly, I did not care, because I have no recollection of it. I do remember walking up to the arena the first day to see the basketball games.

When picking out the tickets, I knew we wouldn't be able to afford a gold-medal game, so that meant not seeing the USA playing, but I did not care. My dad was a pole-vaulter when he was younger, and I was a huge fan of track and field. I felt like these two sports were the best for us to go see. Luckily for me, they were being played during the same week that we were able to go. Within the budget that Dad gave me, we were able to attend the 7th and 8th place women's basketball game and one day of finals for track and field.

I had no clue who might be in that 7th and 8th place game, but I knew without a doubt, it wouldn't be the USA. Our women's basketball team rocks it at the Olympics every four years and 1996 would be no different. They were playing in the gold medal game.

The game we were able to catch was between Japan and Italy. This was the first time I had ever seen an international basketball game in person. International rules are different than what they are in the U.S. The lane is different, the shot clock is different, and the time of the quarters is different. I did not care one bit! I also did not care that I did not know a single player on either team or that our seats were in the rafters. I was watching women's basketball in the OLYPMICS!

The game was late that night and afterward, we were looking for some food. As we were driving to our hotel, which I DO remember was

MY LIFE IN THE 50 STATES

far away from the stadium, we passed a place I had never heard of—Waffle House. Who wouldn't love waffles at midnight? Apparently, everyone does! The place was packed! We were able to get a seat fairly quickly. I had never experienced a Waffle House before and I was quite impressed. The cooks remembered every order that was yelled their way. And if you have never been to a Waffle House, just know that the waitresses really do yell their order to the cook. To this day, it impresses me that they can remember all the orders the way they do. I will also note that in college and graduate school, I spent many other late nights/early mornings in Waffle House.

The next day we were set to see a day of finals and a few prelims of track and field. What made this day even more special was that Sergey Bubka was scheduled to vault. He was the world record holder until 2014. The three of us got to the Olympic Park early to check out the area. Once we wandered around and bought a few souvenirs, we made our way into the stadium.

The budget my dad gave me allowed us to have some of the top seats in the stadium. And I mean *top*, like at the top of the stadium. The way I looked at it, we were able to see every event happening with no problem and we got our exercise climbing all those stairs to our seats. We ended up being in the bowl section of the stadium, which put us on the same end as the long jump pit. This meant we had a great view of Jackie Joyner-Kersee competing in what would be her last Olympic games.

As we settled into our seats, the announcer came over the loud speaker and gave us the only bad news of the trip. Sergey Bubka would not be vaulting because of an injury he sustained at practice prior to the competition. I was really hoping my dad would be able to see him, but unfortunately, it didn't work out that way. He was still excited to be able to watch the pole vault competition.

37

GEORGIA

We watched the marathon racewalking competitors finish their race inside of the stadium, which was really interesting to see. There are rules to racewalking, which make the walkers look very awkward. Racewalkers must keep contact with the ground at all times. This forces them to walk like they are shaking their hips. We also were able to watch some of the prelims for the men's 4x100 relay. This is one of the most exciting races to watch.

Being in the big-bowled section of the stadium turned out to be better than anything I could have imagined. The announcer came over the speakers and announced that Muhammed Ali was in attendance in one of the suites of the stadium. He happened to be in a suite that I could see. When the announcer said he was there, I could see him stand up and wave to the crowd. I saw quite a few famous athletes at the Olympics, but none had the impact on the world of sports and the world as Muhammed Ali.

HAWAII
June 2017

My parents went on a Hawaiian cruise with my aunt Kathleen and uncle Neil the previous year and loved it so much they wanted to take my brother, his family and me to enjoy the same spectacular sites. Because of my schedule as a summer basketball coach, and my sister-in-law's as a school psychologist, the only time we could go was in late June and the cruise was not going to be able to happen. My parents decided that we would still go and visit as many islands as we could, and they put me in charge of creating the itinerary.

I had already been to Pearl Harbor when I coached in California, because the University of Hawaii was in our conference. Since I had to leave a day earlier than everyone else, I scheduled for the tail end of the trip to be on Oahu. Other than Pearl Harbor, I wasn't exactly sure what else we needed to see in Hawaii. So, I did the best research I knew how. I asked my friends on Facebook.

With all of their suggestions, I planned out where we needed to go and what we could see. I sent this to my parents' travel agent and with only about three emails back and forth,

HAWAII

we had a two-week vacation planned out to island hop in Hawaii.

Every island is beautiful in its own way. They are similar, but the way I remember them may be a bit different than how others describe them. Kauai consists of more rain forests and is less inhabited. Think *Jurassic Park*, especially since this is where some of it was filmed.

Hawaii is drier, flat and contains active volcanoes. Maui is the paradise island with the gorgeous sunsets and one of the best sunrises in the world at Haleakala. Oahu is the tourists' island. The main airport in the state of Hawaii is on Oahu, in Honolulu. Pearl Harbor, Iolani Palace and Diamond Head are also in Honolulu; therefore, most tourists flock to the island of Oahu.

We started out on Maui and hit the ground running! One morning, my brother, Scott, his wife, Jessica and I left the hotel at 2:00 a.m. to see the sunrise at Haleakala and then bike down the mountain. Lesson learned here was to pay CLOSE attention to the directions leading you back to your starting point, so you don't have to ride back UP the mountain for about a quarter of a mile because you missed a turn.

The next day, the entire family was able to take the Road to Hana, which was truly breathtaking! This drive takes you all the way around the island of Maui. Every bend we came around, we could hear the rush of water from a waterfall. The natural beauty we saw in person was more majestic than any documentary could ever portray. At the black sand beach, Aiden, my oldest nephew, and I found a cave that led to the ocean. The onyx colored rocks were oval and the size of golf balls at the start of the beach and as you got closer to the water, they became smaller and smaller until they were tiny particles of sand.

MY LIFE IN THE 50 STATES

From the countless waterfalls, the black sand beach and the almost too narrow of a road to be called a road on the side of a cliff, the pictures we have really do not do it justice. I would caution people that this is a bit of a winding road and also takes about 10 hours from pick-up to drop-off. I am normally one who gets motion sickness, but the beauty of this island took my mind off of it completely. It was worth every single minute.

Our last excursion in Maui was snorkeling at Molokini Crater. Well, at least we thought it was going to be. Because we scheduled our dive in the afternoon, the winds were high, and the seas were too rough for the boat to take us out there. The backup plan was to head around the cove to another spot that was full of marine life. Although I didn't see any sea turtles like I wanted to, I did find Dory. No luck on Nemo.

We hopped over to the big island of Hawaii and it was time for some relaxation. I spent a lot of time at my happy place, the beach. I walked out to the water a few times to cool off a bit. It was pretty rocky, and the coral was sharp, so I was very cautious. As I was about to take a step on what I thought was another rock, I looked down and saw the rock move. I almost stepped on a sea turtle. I lost my breath and my balance and tried to run out of the water without falling on the rocks and injuring myself, or an innocent turtle.

After some much needed relaxation, we headed to the island of Kauai. I was looking forward to this island the most, because I was getting to knock something off my bucket list, riding in a helicopter to take a tour of the island. This was quite possibly the best way to see this island. I was like a little kid on Christmas morning. From the moment we pulled up to the airport, I was smiling ear to ear. I didn't even think about the possibility of getting motion sickness.

HAWAII

Our pilot, Marty, was very knowledgeable and gave us some detailed information during the entire trip. We learned where blockbuster hits such as *Indiana Jones: Raiders of the Lost Ark* with Harrison Ford and *The Descendants* with George Clooney, were filmed on the island. The Robinson family owns almost 52,000 acres on the island and has one of the most famous waterfalls on their property. Manawaiopuna Falls is the waterfall that was featured in the first *Jurassic Park*. In fact, Bruce Robinson's helicopter was the one that was used in the movie for that scene. Mr. Robinson still lives on the top of the mountains, at the edge with an ocean view, and occasionally uses the helicopter to get from his house down the mountain.

We flew around the rest of the island, coming up on Waipi'o Valley (also known as The Valley of the Kings), which looks like a series of kings' thrones naturally made into the mountainside. This led us to the Na Pali coastline to see the beaches and reefs. Something that is very rare is that there are no private beaches on the island of Kauai. Everyone has access to every beach on the island.

The helicopter ride was everything I expected and more. Touring an island from the sky just gives you an entirely different perspective of the beauty that nature has provided us with. This ride is why Kauai is my favorite Hawaiian island.

Our final stop was Oahu. Visiting this island was different for me because I had been here before. I did get to visit a few new places, along with returning to Pearl Harbor. When I was coaching at San Jose State, I visited the Arizona Memorial with our sports information director, but it was a very quick trip, since we needed to get back in order to catch our flight. This time with my family, we went through the museum and watched the videos.

MY LIFE IN THE 50 STATES

Then it was time to take the short boat ride over to the memorial. It baffles me that after all these years there is still oil in the water from the ship. My mom had visited the memorial when she was very young and at the age of 75, she was able to visit it again. My mom was also born four days after it was bombed.

My family had the opportunity to visit the Iolani Palace. This palace is the only palace that is on US soil. It has a very unique story to it. The last queen of Hawaii, Queen Liliuokalani, was actually imprisoned in a bedroom on the top floor of the palace for eight months. The palace is now a National Historic Landmark and filled with the furniture, paintings and china that the monarchy used over 100 years ago.

After a couple of full days touring the island, the rest of my family was content on sleeping in. However, I wanted to hike Diamond Head before I flew home. Diamond Head is an inactive volcano on the edge of Oahu. There is a panoramic view of the island from the top. It was one of the best views of any of the islands. The key is making the hike up to the top. The trail is fairly steep and there are two sets of stairs with one having almost 100 steps and the other 76. I decided this was my workout for the day. Waking up at sunrise was worth the view from the top. In fact, I am not sure there was a bad view the entire two weeks we were in Hawaii.

IDAHO
March 2001

DURING MY FINAL YEAR at Arkansas, we were able to go dancing in the NCAA tournament. March Madness is the most exciting three weeks of college basketball. The upsets that happen. The number of games being played all day. Cinderella stories. It is a basketball lover's dream! This tournament, we were sent to Boise, Idaho, to take on Georgetown.

Arkansas was the #7 seed and Georgetown was #10. This was one of those matchups in the NCAA tournament that always makes for a close game. Just because you are seeded higher, doesn't mean you are a shoe-in to win. Georgetown was a great program and would test our young team. A few minutes into the game, the horn malfunctioned and would not turn off for a good five minutes. Think about that—a loud, obnoxious horn continuously going off. It was finally fixed, and play resumed.

We were known as a defensive pressure team, so we turned up the heat. Our offense, even with future NBA All-Star Joe Johnson, could not seem to get going. It was back and forth the entire first half and Georgetown took a one-point lead into halftime. Apparently, the horn was not fixed completely, and the

IDAHO

table officials had to use a hand-held air horn to let officials know about substitutions.

The second half was back and forth just like the first. Neither team could get going on the offensive end and it was coming down to the end. With 35.8 seconds left in the game, Georgetown had the ball. The shot clock in a men's college basketball game is 35 seconds. This means that a player has to shoot the ball and it must hit the rim before the horn goes off at 35 seconds. With time winding down, Georgetown guard, Nathaniel Burton, drove down the left side of the lane and Arkansas fans, Coach Richardson and even Burton himself, believe he got the shot off as the buzzer was going off, which means he did not get it off in time. The entire Georgetown fan base thought otherwise. They all celebrated in the stands as if he did and his teammates mobbed him under the basket.

The referees went to the monitor for a review. The anticipation to wait and see if they were going to count the basket or wave it off to send us to overtime was intense. A few moments later, one of the referees made the signal to count the basket. Our hearts dropped. The guys walked into the locker room in disbelief. We were going home.

We had to wait for the post-game interviews, which are mandatory by the NCAA. It makes the waiting more excruciating. The players and coaches finally loaded the bus and we headed back to the hotel to wait and see when our flight would leave. If your team does not advance in the NCAA tournament and your game started before 2:00 p.m., you would head home immediately. When we got back to the hotel, all of our fans and the band gathered in the lobby to welcome us back. Although we lost, the fans erupted in cheer as if we had won. It was technically an upset, and that's what makes March Madness so mad.

ILLINOIS
March 2014

In 2014, I was in my fourth year coaching at Stephen F. Austin in Nacogdoches, Texas. We were the Southland Conference Champions, but unfortunately, fell short of going to the NCAA tournament. We chose to play in the WBI, Women's Basketball Invitational Tournament, which is one of the three post-season tournaments for women's college basketball. We hosted the first couple of rounds, but then had to go to Charleston, South Carolina, for the semifinals.

After beating College of Charleston, we had to scramble to arrange for us to fly to Chicago to take on the University of Illinois at Chicago. We had to figure all of that out in the span of an hour. Lucky for us, our director of basketball operations, Todd Stutzman, got it all figured out.

A group of us flew to Chicago on the first flight out in the morning and two more groups followed on two additional flights. It was a very quick turnaround. We played Friday night, flew out Saturday and had the championship game Sunday at 2:00 p.m. Once the entire crew got to Chicago, we went to the gym and had a light practice, a shake-your-travel-legs-out type of practice.

ILLINOIS

We were able to go over a few of the sets UIC runs and give a few tidbits on the players for the game that night.

When we got back to the hotel, we had a nice catered meal in one of the ballrooms of the hotel. After eating we went over our scouting report of UIC, watched some game film from their previous games and called it a night. We were all pretty exhausted. Some of us had a 3:00 a.m. wakeup call that morning and the players were worn out from the previous games.

Every night before road games one of the other assistants and I would collect cell phones from the players at 11:00 p.m. We did this in order to insure there was not any late-night texting, face timing or anything else distracting the night before a game. If there was ever an emergency, players' families knew they could call any of us coaches. This night our players had all the phones turned in by 9:30 p.m.

The next morning, we had our pregame meal, watched some more film and prepared for our final game of the season. I was one of the first people on the bus and saw one of our juniors, Daylyn Harris, looking in all the seats. She looked a bit frazzled. I asked her what was going on and she told me she was looking for her knee brace. She had left it on the bus after practice the night before. In any other town this would have been ok, because we kept the same bus. However, in Chicago, we were not on the same bus. We tried to figure out where the other bus was, but for some reason, the company could not track it down. Daylyn was one of our starters and a big contributor in different aspects of the game for us. Unfortunately, she was unavailable for us that day.

We struggled in the first half, but somehow came from being down to taking a 2-point lead into halftime. We were being out-rebounded and rebounding was something we took pride

MY LIFE IN THE 50 STATES

in. It seemed as if the travel was starting to catch up to everyone. To start the second half, UIC went on a run and we could never recover. The score was as close as two points, but fatigue set in. Porsha Roberts, our leading scorer, did just that and led us with 21 points. The season didn't end the way we wanted, but we did set a record for the historic program. That team is the only team in program history to win three post-season games. That is something to be proud of.

We celebrated with the players, our administration and support staff at the world-famous Giordano's Pizza. If you have never had Chicago deep-dish pizza, this one is a must try! Even though we had lost, dinner was upbeat, and everyone seemed to be excited about what we had accomplished that year.

The following morning, we flew back to Houston and hopped on the bus for the two-hour drive back to Nacogdoches. As we pulled into the south of town, a police escort met us.

Like most college athletes, our players were asleep on the bus until they heard the police sirens. A few of them thought we were in trouble. The word passed to the back that it was an escort for us back to the gym. The players were even more excited to see the group of fans, some of the men's basketball staff and administrators waiting to welcome us back home. It was a tough way to end our season, but that team and season was a special one to me.

INDIANA
July 2009

How appropriate was it that basketball took me to the Hoosier state? One summer during the recruiting period in July, my schedule and the Adidas circuit took me to Bloomington, Indiana. It was going to be a quick turnaround for me, but I was excited that some of the games were being played on the campus of Indiana University at Assembly Hall. At this time, the NCAA allowed summer tournaments to be held on the campuses of universities.

A few years later, this would not be allowed. I understand it provided somewhat of a recruiting edge for that university to have all of those players visit their campus, but what it took away for people like me was the opportunity to visit historic gymnasiums.

Assembly Hall is where Hall of Fame coach, Bob Knight, coached his Indiana Hoosiers for 29 years. He was famous for his short temper with players and officials. In fact, during one home game against in-state rival Purdue, he was so upset with a series of calls by the officials that he received a technical foul. Naturally, he was irate with this call. He let his emotions get the best of him and threw a chair from his bench across the floor as the Purdue

INDIANA

player was about to shoot the technical free throw. This earned him his second technical and an automatic seat in the locker room for the remainder of the game. If you ever get the chance, google this incident. It was only 5 minutes into the game when this happened.

When preparing to watch games at a tournament with hundreds of teams, a coach must make a grid of all the games with the court number and time of game. Being organized is key to summer recruiting. At least it was for me. Once the schedule came out, I was hoping that I was going to be able to catch at least ONE game in Assembly Hall. As it turned out, I was going to catch...one game.

I was very excited and eager to be able to be in such a historic basketball gym. I remember walking in the gym and down the tunnel. It was almost as if I was walking back in time. It looked just like it did every time I saw it on television. Not really sure if I was expecting it to look different, but the feeling of being in there is what gave me goose bumps.

Besides the chair-throwing incident, there were quite a few historic basketball moments that occurred there. The Rolling Stones and Elton John have even performed there.

I felt as if I had a bucket list item checked off my list, even though I really didn't have a list at that time. I still had a basketball game to watch. Even though I was coaching at a school in California, I would still watch several Texas basketball teams, because I had so many connections to the state I am from. I went to watch a team from the Austin area called TeamXpress. Longhorn great, Clarissa Davis-Wrightsil was the coach at the time. I remember being very impressed by a long, lanky 5'10" wing player who had a great jump shot and the wingspan of a

MY LIFE IN THE 50 STATES

6'2" post player. I made sure to mark her down and get her on the mailing list.

The following year I made sure to keep up with her progress, but I had a feeling she didn't want to come all the way to California. Just so happens, at the end of that year, I left California and went to coach at Stephen F. Austin in Nacogdoches, Texas.

We ended up signing Tierany Henderson, that long lanky guard and her jump shot turned into a great 3-point shot. Tierany was one of seven signees we had that year at SFA who helped us win two conference championships and advance to the WBI Championship I talked about in Illinois and the WNIT the following year. I'm glad I was in Bloomington that summer.

IOWA
January 2017

WHILE I WAS OUT of coaching, I decided I wanted to use this time to travel as much as possible. One of the bucket list items was to travel to all 50 states by the time I was 50. There were a few states that I had absolutely NO CLUE as to how or why I would go visit them, one of those states being Iowa. I knew three people that lived there: a former player, a coaching friend and his wife. That was it for the entire state. The likelihood of me going to visit them was slim. So, I needed to figure out how I was going to make a trip to Iowa.

As the basketball season was progressing, I would keep up with my close coaching friends and their basketball schedules to see how they were doing, especially in conference. When I checked in on Kansas, it dawned on me that they play Iowa State in the Big 12 Conference.

I believe timing is everything and it proved perfect timing here. They were set to play at Iowa State the following week. I researched the route on google maps and it was only 460 miles from my house to Ames. A six-hour road trip was a walk in the park for someone like me. I texted my good friend, Damitria

IOWA

Buchanan, an assistant for Kansas, and told her I was coming to the game. Like most people, she asked, "Why Iowa State?" I said, "Why not?"

I started the drive from Fayetteville, and like most of my road trips, I got lost in the zone of driving. Driving long distance has been my thing since I started driving. Shortly after getting my permit, I helped my parents drive from Arizona to Texas. This was also shortly after learning how to drive a stick shift. I was six hours from home during the time I went to junior college at Odessa College.

When I transferred to the University of Arkansas, I was ten and a half hours from my hometown of Kenedy, Texas, where my grandmother still lived, and I was 15 hours from my parents in Rural Hall, North Carolina. Every long distance road trip, I had plenty of music to blast, several packs of gum and Diet Dr. Pepper. By the time I took my Ames road trip, I didn't drink much Diet Dr. Pepper unless it was late, and I needed a quick pick-me-up.

Once I got to Ames, I was able to visit with all of my former coworkers. When they had their film session with the team, I went upstairs and settled in. Damitria came by the room when they were finished and we were able to catch up and per usual, she had me rolling and in tears from laughter. She is by far one of the funniest people I know, and you put her with her former teammate and former coworker, Aqua Franklin, it's hard to not laugh at these two.

The game was at 2:00 p.m. on Sunday. I was able to get in a quick workout at the hotel before getting ready and finding a lunch spot. I looked outside the windows and the sun was shining, it was a gorgeous day! I packed up my belongings, checked out of the hotel and headed to the car. When I walked through the hotel

MY LIFE IN THE 50 STATES

doors, I felt like I was slapped in the face with a lie. That beautiful sunny day was one of the coldest and windiest I had experienced up to that time in my life. The wind was strong, and it just made the cold air feel colder. This south Texas girl isn't a fan of temperatures below her age.

I made my way to the arena early, so I could get as close of a parking spot as I could. Having been in college athletics, I knew that since I didn't have a parking pass, it wasn't going to be very close. I talked with the parking attendants to determine which gate I needed to go to for the pass list.

I wanted the shortest route possible because of that cold wind. As I walked as fast as I could to get out of the bitter cold, I saw a little girl in a dress, no leggings, no jacket and a long sleeve shirt on. I didn't want to judge her parents, so I just gave them a mean side eye as I walked as fast as my legs would go in order to pass them. It was 20-something degrees, wind chill was too cold to even mention, and this little girl had bare legs.

Hilton Coliseum is a tough place for opponents to play—men or women. Iowa State women are known for their shooting abilities. The game was going to be tough, but hey, you never know! Unfortunately, KU dropped that game at Hilton. After the game, I said good-bye, hopped in my car and headed south. I honestly do not remember much about the drive home except I was able to see a beautiful sunset on I-35.

KANSAS
June 2000

AFTER ABOUT THREE MONTHS OF working as a student athletic trainer for the men's basketball program at Arkansas, I decided I wanted to coach more than I wanted to be a trainer. I saw the passion that Coach Nolan Richardson had for coaching and that was the way I felt about basketball.

As I stated in Arkansas, I confided in Coach A about wanting to coach and he advised me to work basketball camps in the summertime. I decided to look up how many schools were within an eight-hour drive from Fayetteville, looked up all camp dates and organized them on a calendar. Once I decided which schools I could drive to, I emailed the coach who, according to their school biography, was in charge of camp, and just asked if I could work camp.

The first response I received back was from Maggie Mahood. She was the director of basketball operations for women's basketball at the University of Kansas. I was so excited that someone needed me to come work camp! Soon after, I received emails from Louisiana Tech, Arkansas State and Vanderbilt. I couldn't believe the responses I got back.

KANSAS

Since this was long before GPS was even thought of, I had to make sure I had my atlas in my car along with printed-out directions to each school. Kansas would be the first basketball camp I would work at for another school. I had already worked the men's and women's camps at Arkansas, but I was very nervous. One thing that many people don't know about me (and are very surprised to hear) is that I get so much anxiety about going somewhere I have never been before. Yes, the woman who has been to all 50 states and traveled to Europe and Africa gets anxiety about going somewhere new.

According to MapQuest and my trusty atlas, it was going to take me four hours to get to Lawrence, Kansas. We were supposed to have a camp coaches meeting at 10:00 a.m. on Sunday morning, then registration for camp would begin at noon and we would start it all off at 3:00 p.m. I was so nervous about missing my alarm that I did not sleep very much and ended up leaving 30 minutes early.

The drive was fairly easy, with some parts of the trip on two-lane highways and some on interstate. As I exited on Highway 10 towards Lawrence, I started thinking about all of the basketball history at Kansas. James Naismith, the inventor of basketball, founded the men's basketball program at Kansas. Phog Allen Fieldhouse is one of the best venues in college basketball. Lynette Woodard, the first female Harlem Globetrotter, played at Kansas. I was about to stand in the same gym where some of the greatest basketball players in history played. Chills.

I pulled up to Naismith Hall about 20 minutes early. I am always paranoid about showing up to the wrong place, so I parked my car facing the door to see if the people walking in the door at least looked like they were about to do SOMETHING with basketball. I

60

MY LIFE IN THE 50 STATES

was always taught that being early is to be on time, to be on time is to be late and to be late is to be left. I am always on time. I made sure I went in at 9:50 a.m. Thankfully, I was in the right spot.

Our meeting was full of introductions, rules, assignments and itineraries. We had just a few minutes before registration was about to begin, so I decided to move all my belongings inside to my dorm room. Registration began with a rush of young campers and their parents dragging sleeping bags and suitcases and carrying cases of water. Before we headed over to the fieldhouse, everyone was to meet outside in the parking lot. I forgot my coaching notebook upstairs, so I hopped on the elevator with a group of campers.

A young camper, maybe in the third or fourth grade, looked up at me and in the most innocent voice asked, "Are you going to be my coach and teach me how to play basketball?" That's when it hit me. "Why yes, I am," I answered. I will never forget the way I felt when she asked me that. My heart knew I was in the right spot and doing what I was supposed to do.

KENTUCKY
March 2003

IN APRIL OF 2002, Coach Mike Anderson had been named the head coach at University of Alabama-Birmingham. I was a graduate assistant coach at the University of Montevallo, which is 20 minutes south of Birmingham. The conference tournament for Conference USA was being held in Louisville, Kentucky, at Freedom Hall. This was the home court for the University of Louisville.

I had class and internship responsibilities the week of the tournament. And in all honesty, the chances of UAB (as the #8 seed) making the tournament championship were slim. Yvonne, Coach A and Marcheita's youngest daughter, was the only one of the children who made the trip to the tournament. Darcheita, the oldest Anderson, stayed in Birmingham with the other children, Michael, Jr., and Suney, and her 10-month-old daughter, Aiyana. We all resorted to watching the tournament games on TV.

The team made a surprising run to the semi-final game, defeating the #1 seed and #8-ranked Marquette in the quarter-finals. As the semi-final game against #4 seed St. Louis played on television, Darcheita and I were on the phone commentating

KENTUCKY

to each other. The boys played tough and things started to look promising that they would win and play in the championship game on Sunday. We started to do the math. If they won, we would have enough time to load up the car with everyone and drive the six hours through the night and arrive in Louisville in time to catch the championship game at noon against host #4 seed and #20 Louisville.

We agreed that when the game ended, I would throw an overnight bag in my car and drive to meet them in Birmingham. The clock struck 00:00 and I quickly hung up the phone. I couldn't believe we were going to do it. I loved a good road trip. Six hours through the night to watch the championship game in Freedom Hall was worth it.

I don't remember much of the actual trip up there. I know between Darcheita, Michael and I, we made the drive go by pretty quick. Luckily, Aiyana slept most of the way, as did Suney. We rolled into Louisville just past 7:00 a.m. I was exhausted. The adrenaline rush was over, and I just wanted some sleep. We all walked into the suite as the rest of the family was waking up. Breakfast was about to be served, but I just wanted the bed. I am not too sure who went to eat and who slept. I just crashed.

The championship game was a close one the entire time. Going into halftime, UAB had a one-point lead. In the second half, Louisville made a push and was able to keep the lead for the rest of the half. UAB was able to cut it to one with under a minute to go, but a bad shot and a loose ball out of bounds on them forced them to foul and time just ran out. Playing four games in four days is a tough feat for anyone. It was all worth it. Seeing a game of that caliber in a gym that historic was worth the little sleep and long drive.

64

LOUISIANA
July 2005

I HAD HEARD MANY STORIES about New Orleans. The food, Bourbon Street and a basketball tournament called Battle on the Bayou. The month of July is a big month of recruiting for college coaches. This is the month the NCAA allows coaches to watch basketball tournaments outside of the high school season. I had always wanted to go to New Orleans for all of the previous listed reasons and was hopeful that basketball would somehow take me there.

The summer of 2005, my head coach at Tyler Junior College, Trenia Tillis Hoard, was making a plan for where I needed to go recruiting in July. I would strongly suggest to her that I should go to New Orleans because it was the biggest tournament with the most players we were recruiting. I tried not to make it obvious I wanted to go down there for the food and Bourbon Street as well as the tournament. As luck would have it, it worked out that I would make the seven-hour drive from East Texas to New Orleans in July.

Junior colleges have little to no budget, so I always ended up staying with a friend who was coaching at a bigger budget school. I would also photocopy the book that was full of rosters. These books can range from $250–$700. It's RIDICULOUS!! This

LOUISIANA

is frustrating for schools with smaller budgets, especially when some of the information is incorrect, but that is an entirely different book to be written. I would figure out a way to see the tournament on our own budget.

Since my friend was at a school with a limitless budget, I was able to stay at the Marriott on Canal Street. This hotel was centrally located to food and entertainment. Oh, and it wasn't too far from the gym. I spent my days driving between the Pontchartrain Center and the Alario Center watching games. When there was a blowout game, most of the coaches planned where they were going to eat for the night. Food is a high priority when coaches are on the road recruiting.

I knew a few people in the coaching world by this point and I had arranged to meet some of them for dinner. I am not sure how, but I ended up at the casino and then walking down Bourbon. I also don't know how many Hurricanes (popular cocktail drink on Bourbon Street) I had. Throughout the night I was introduced to more coaches, but the Hurricanes really affected my memory on exactly whom I met. Once I realized it was almost 2:00 a.m. and I had a 9:00 a.m. game I needed to watch and then head back to Tyler, I found my way back to the Marriot and passed out. Even at the age of 27, going out on Bourbon the night before you are supposed to watch games and then drive home for seven hours was not the smartest thing to do.

Not sure how I did it, but I made the game on time. The drive home was way more difficult than it needed to be. I had to take several stops along the way to catch some quick catnaps. My experience in New Orleans was one I will never forget and I'm so grateful I had it when I did. Later that summer, on August 23rd, Hurricane Katrina hit the city and New Orleans was never the same.

MAINE
August 2016

THE SUMMER OF 2016 WAS an eventful one. At the beginning of August, I was able to travel with the Arkansas Razorbacks men's basketball team to Spain on their foreign tour. Spain was always on my bucket list and I got to experience Madrid, Valencia and Barcelona with some amazing people. There was a conference in Hartford, Connecticut, that I really wanted to go to, and it was three days after I returned from Spain. My plan was to go to the conference and then drive through several other New England area states.

I made my way to Portland, Maine. I wanted to get some exercise as I took in the sights, so I found a trail by one of the most photographed lighthouses on the east coast. It was a beautiful day and I just wanted to soak it all in that I was in MAINE!!! A south Texas girl was all the way up in MAINE!

Prior to Spain, I had sent off my sample to have my DNA tested. Since I am adopted, I did not know any of my medical history, nor did I know my race or ethnicity. I was not searching out my biological family for some storybook reunion. I only wanted to know my ethnic background and to see if I was predisposed to any major diseases.

MAINE

As I was walking along the path to the lighthouse, I stopped to watch a painter painting the ocean views. That is when my email alert went off. My DNA results were in. My heart dropped. I didn't know what to expect. I didn't know how I was going to feel. Should I check it while I was by myself? Should I wait to go back to the hotel and check it? The answer to that last question was an obvious "No," because I wasn't patient enough to wait. I decided I would sit down, take a deep breath and open it up.

My heart was racing. So many questions would be answered, but were new questions going to arise? The question that was answered was where my ancestors are from. I took a moment to take it all in because I knew that I would forever remember exactly where I was when these questions were answered.

I opened the email and, of course, the Internet was slow. Finally, I was able to see my results. I am 37.1% Portuguese and Spanish. I am 17.1% Native American. 23andMe categorizes Native American as the native peoples from North, Central or South America and they narrow it down for you. Mine was narrowed down to Mexico. It also told me that I had someone in my biological family who was born in two of these three countries within the last 200 years before coming to the United States.

The other largest percentage was Broadly Southern European at 19.3%. This includes the Iberian, Italian and Balkan peninsulas. According to 23andMe, Broadly Southern European DNA matches several specific populations and is difficult to assign to just one.

Wow. I don't know if I was shocked or not. I looked up at the waves crashing on the rocks, the beaming sun hitting my legs and the cool ocean breeze coming in off the coast. I cannot describe it, but I knew I had some sort of mix of ethnicity. It won't make

MY LIFE IN THE 50 STATES

sense to the majority of you reading this, but that is ok. I knew for me, it was something different. Now I had proof that it wasn't all in my head. As I did some more digging into the results, and some of the lists of biological relatives, it was determined that I am definitely Hispanic and my biological parents were Mexican American. I finally had the answers I had been wanting.

I had another part of the test still to look up, what genetic medical conditions I was predisposed to. This made me just as nervous. Was it in my DNA for Parkinson's? Heart disease? Was I going to die young? I took another deep breath, prayed and clicked on the link for the medical history. I had ZERO genetic variances for any life-threatening or life-altering diseases. I did have the markers for Celiac disease, which is a disorder in which eating gluten can trigger the immune system and affect the small intestine. I can deal with that.

After reading these results, I cried a few tears. So much relief came out with a simple email. I sat on that bench, watched the waves, listened to nature happening around me and thanked God for giving me the life He did, allowing MY parents, John and Diane Greve to raise me alongside MY brother, Scott. You see, blood only makes you related. It doesn't make you family. I took one more deep breath and then it was time for a lobster roll.

MARYLAND
October 2005

In the fall of 2005, my best friend was getting married. Gigi and I had known each other since we attended Odessa College together and then went on to Arkansas together. She was set to marry Chris Johnson on October 8th in Maryland near her parents' home. She went to high school in Virginia, but her parents moved to Maryland after she graduated college.

I flew into Baltimore on Thursday in order to be there for all of the festivities on Friday. Gigi's mom, Vera, had planned a bridal shower at a restaurant on the water for Friday. This would allow for her bridesmaids and women in her family to attend. The majority of us were coming from out of state, so the timing of this made more sense. It was a simple and enjoyable lunch filled with presents and stories about the bride-to-be.

That evening we had the rehearsal dinner at the church. Gigi's father, Everett, Sr., was a pastor and had his own church. However, it was in a storefront, and she wanted a traditional church wedding. She was able to have it at her sister-in-law, Delores's, church, Coventry Church. It also had a great area for the dinner portion, which meant there was no need to rent out another place.

MARYLAND

After the rehearsal, Gigi, another bridesmaid, Ebony and I headed to the hotel we had reserved for the night. We were getting ready to settle in for the night and Ebony called Gigi to her room. When we got there, she told Gigi not to freak out, which automatically makes a bride freak out the night before her wedding. There was some sort of flood in Ebony's room and her bridesmaid's dress was wet. Ebony already had a plan for how she was going to handle it. She had already looked up a dry cleaner and was going to have it there first thing in the morning, and it would be ready in time for the wedding.

We still had a problem. Ebony wasn't able to stay in her room any more. Gigi's friend from high school, Janet, had originally made the reservations, so she called the hotel to see what she was able to do for us. Unfortunately, there wasn't anything the hotel could do, since it was sold out. We packed up her stuff and moved it into our room and had a big sleepover.

It's wedding day! That morning, Ebony left early in order to get her dress to a dry cleaners, so she would have it in time for the wedding. Gigi and I ate some breakfast, packed up our room and headed to the church. Since the church was in Washington, D.C., Gigi wanted all of us at the church by 1:00 p.m. to start getting ready. The wedding didn't start until 5:00 p.m., but the D.C. area traffic is so unpredictable.

We spent a better part of four hours preparing ourselves for the wedding and helping Gigi transform into the beautiful bride that she was. Her niece, Elyse, was the cutest flower girl with her white dress that had rose petals in the tulle skirt. The rest of the bridesmaids were doing hair, makeup and, of course, eating. Once we made our transformations, the only thing left we had to do was marry this young lady off.

MY LIFE IN THE 50 STATES

The ceremony was simply beautiful. Gigi decided the bridesmaids would walk down the aisle with their partners. Except me. I was walking down the aisle by myself. I was so incredibly nervous. I am such a klutz. I have managed to trip over the lines on a basketball court in tennis shoes. What could possibly happen with me walking down a carpeted aisle with four-inch heels on? I wanted Gigi and Chris to have memories of their wedding and did not want it to include me falling down the aisle. I held my breath, made my abs tight to help with my balance and prayed I would make it. Sure enough, I made it.

It was a family affair for the people who performed as Gigi walked down the aisle. Her uncle, Errol Cooper, sang "You Are So Beautiful." His voice filled the church; he didn't even need the microphone. Pastor Rochelle Richardson officiated the ceremony and made it memorable for Chris and Gigi. Chris's cousin, Lauren Bullock, sang as well. The praise dancer, Jennifer, was also one of Gigi's nieces' godmother. Sadly, Jennifer passed away three years ago from that dreaded disease ... cancer.

After the "I do's," we gathered to take photos and then headed to the Jaycee Center in Oxon Hill, Maryland, for the reception. The reception hall had a great setup because we were able to eat upstairs and then go for dancing and fun downstairs. Being the maid of honor, I was tasked with giving a speech. I knew I would get emotional, but had no idea my eyes would become Niagara Falls, and I would get so choked up.

Gigi and I were each other's only family when we were in college. Her family was in Virginia and mine in North Carolina and Texas. I spoke about how she always had me as her plus-one for events when we were in college and how much it meant to me. Family doesn't always mean you are related. And we were family. I

73

MARYLAND

am not sure how much everyone could actually understand what I was saying for the toast, but they clapped and cheered anyway.

After dinner we headed downstairs and went to party! Before the wedding, Gigi told me that when she would throw her bouquet, she was going to turn around and throw it right at me. Even though I knew she wanted me to catch it, I didn't take her to mean it literally.

When it was that time, all the single women gathered behind her waiting for her to toss the bouquet. Someone counted to three, Gigi acted as if she is going to throw it over her shoulder, turned around, looked me in the eye and threw it right to me.

Just as I was clinching my fingers around the flowers, I saw a long arm stretch in and grab it from my hands. It happened so fast; I didn't have time to react. I looked up and one of Chris's athletes from Penn State, Dominique Blake, had snatched it from my hands. I couldn't do anything else but crack up. I looked at Gigi and we cried laughing. Some things just weren't meant to be.

MASSACHUSETTS
August 2016

As a kid, my brother and I would record movies from TV on a VHS tape, so we could watch them whenever we wanted to. One of my all-time favorite movies was *Splash*, starring Tom Hanks and Daryl Hannah. It is about a man who finds a mermaid off the coast of Cape Cod. Ever since I had watched that movie, I had always wanted to go to Cape Cod. When I planned out my New England road trip, I made sure I would stay a few days on the beach on the Cape.

When I got to Cape Cod, I knew the only thing I wanted to do was enjoy the beach. I pulled up to my hotel and as I checked in, I asked about the best beach to visit. That's all I wanted. Well, that and some good seafood.

I didn't pack my usual beach items because I didn't have room for them. Before heading to dinner, I found a store to find at least a nice beach towel, so I wouldn't have to swipe one from the hotel. Being from the south, I am used to Walmart being EVERYWHERE. Well, on the Cape, there is no Walmart. I did find another store that was supposed to have beach necessities. I am not sure if it was because it was already August or what, but this store only had

MASSACHUSETTS

a small section of towels and nothing else for the beach. I grabbed a towel and headed to dinner.

The local spot I found was quite interesting. The bar was decorated with fireman patches on the wall, ceiling and any other open space. I honestly do not remember the name of the restaurant. I wish I did because it deserves its recognition for the atmosphere and vibe it had. The food was good, but nothing extraordinary.

I ate rather quickly because I wanted to see the beach at sunset. The woman at the front desk had told me Smuggler's Beach is where I should go. I followed my GPS and drove around looking for the best spot to take a picture. I may have ended up further down from Smuggler's Beach than I intended. However, the spot I found was an amazing shot. It was so perfect; I was waiting for the mermaid to come out of the water.

The next morning, I got up early enough to do a small workout in my room, so I could get to the beach as soon as possible. I headed to Smuggler's Beach and found a spot to relax.

Being on the beach in Massachusetts was so different than the beach in Texas, there was very little humidity. There was, what seemed like, gale force winds in Massachusetts. The heat is not felt on the east coast like it is felt in Texas. Regardless, any beach is my happy place. I fulfilled a dream I had since I was seven years old, to relax on the beach in Cape Cod. Checked off two items on the bucket list with this visit.

MICHIGAN
November 2017

OH MY GOODNESS!! I finished a four-state road trip and only had ONE state left. I shared most of my travels on social media and revealed that my final state to travel to was Michigan. One of my good coaching friends that I have known since I got into coaching years ago, Fred Castro, reached out to me and said I should come visit him and his family. I could catch one of his games (he is the head coach at Eastern Michigan University) and knock off my final state. Now if you remember, I wanted to hit all 50 states before I was 50, and it was beginning to look like I would hit all 50 by the end of 2017.

I started to look at his game schedule as well as my schedule for the year and determined it would work great for me to fly up for the first game of the season. Eastern Michigan is located in Yspilanti (pronounced ĭp·sĭ·lăn′·tē), a short 25-minute drive from the Detroit airport. Being a frequent flyer, I had just enough miles to use for the quick trip to Michigan.

I am not sure what exactly I was expecting from Michigan, besides cold weather. I grabbed an Uber from the airport and met Fred at the university just in time for practice. Even though I

MICHIGAN

was out of college coaching, I was still excited to watch practices and learn from other coaches. He gave me a tour of the facilities, which far exceeded my expectations.

Many people tend to think smaller schools are not as nice or do not have facilities as good as some of the larger schools. Eastern Michigan proves those people wrong. The basketball team has a practice gym, a state of the art weight room, a nutrition station for pre and post workout snacks for the athletes and an amazing arena to play in.

Practice was fairly short since it was the day before a game. You could tell the players were eager to play someone other than their teammates. After practice, Fred and I hopped in the car to meet his wife and kids for dinner. We had an early night because the game the following day was an early one.

Women's basketball programs around the country have a great initiative with elementary schools. Schools will have some sort of competition or program where students must qualify to be able to go to a basketball game during a school day. These programs expose children to women's college basketball, which is a great benefit. The game I chose to attend was the elementary school day for Eastern Michigan. This also means being in a gym with about two thousand screaming, screeching children.

On game day, Cindy (Fred's wife) and I headed up to the gym for the noon tip-off. The game was exciting, and the girls pulled off the victory over Florida A&M, 83–61. Winning makes it better. That evening, Cindy, Fred and I went to a chophouse in Ann Arbor, the home of the University of Michigan, which is only 20 minutes away. I had no idea that so many things were so close in proximity in Michigan. Being from Texas always has my sense of proximity off. Most cities are usually two to three hours apart, not 20–30 minutes.

MY LIFE IN THE 50 STATES

The following day, Fred had to hit the road recruiting at a high school tournament with one of his assistant coaches. My flight was scheduled for 2:00 p.m., so there wasn't time for me to see much. Cindy was gracious enough to drive me to Detroit and then drive me around town. We passed Comerica Park where the Detroit Tigers play. Historic Fox Theater is just down the street from the park. The city of Detroit is working hard to revitalize the downtown area.

Other than getting to see my good friends and being able to complete my 50 states bucket list, this trip was not as exciting as the other states I visited. Had I been more patient that fall, I would have still been able to complete my goal.

In March of 2018, for the NCAA men's basketball tournament, I traveled to Detroit to watch Arkansas play in the round of 64. I am glad I was able to go back because I had time to visit the original home of Motown Records, the legendary record label started by Berry Gordy, Jr. It all worked out better than I could have planned.

MINNESOTA
October 2017

ON THIS FOUR-STATE ROAD TRIP, I wanted to take a picture of myself at each of the state lines. This would have been a great idea to start years ago, but better late than never, right? I was able to get the picture as I crossed into Wisconsin, but when I crossed into Minnesota, there was not a rest stop or welcome center on the state line. This was pretty upsetting, but I kept on to Minneapolis.

To be honest, the only places I knew about in Minneapolis before this trip were the Mall of America and the University of Minnesota. Before I left for my trip, I emailed one of the assistants at Minnesota to see if I would be able to watch some workouts while I was there. I always find a way to fit basketball into my trips. It just so happened to be the first day of official practice. I also googled "things to do" in Minneapolis and found a beautiful waterfall that was smack dab in the middle of the metropolitan city.

I planned to stay at an Airbnb, just as I did in Wisconsin. The house was only about 10 minutes from the Mall of America, and let's be honest, this is the real reason I stayed in Minneapolis. I am

MINNESOTA

not much of a shopper, but could I really pass up the opportunity to shop here? Heck no! The Mall of America is large enough that an adult could get lost. There are over 500 stores. Before I arrived in Minneapolis, I looked up the map of the mall and was happy to find out the majority of the stores I wanted to go to were all located in the same wing.

Since I was arriving several hours before my check-in to my Airbnb, I went to the mall first. This trip to the mall proved to be more beneficial than I would realize. I would figure that out once I got to South Dakota. I spent a few hours wandering and shopping, grabbed some dinner and headed to the Airbnb for the night.

The next morning, I had planned to workout, but the bed was holding me hostage. I wanted to stop at the waterfall I found on my google search, called Minnehaha Falls, which was located in the middle of the city. There was a trail along the creek that the falls run from, so I decided walking would be the workout for the day.

It was an overcast day, with a small chance of rain. I took the chance it wouldn't rain on my parade. The waterfall was from what seemed like a slow-moving creek. However, the power of the rushing water from the waterfall was enough to spray me from the lookout. It was no Niagara Falls, however, it was very powerful and dominant. This time I was able to find a nice young lady to take my picture in front of the falls.

After my walk, I headed towards the University of Minnesota. I planned to grab some lunch somewhere close to the gym and walk to practice. I have seen many pictures of the university athletic facilities, but the majority of them were covered in snow. It was slightly odd not to see any snow, even if it was only early October. After lunch I headed over to Williams Arena to watch the women practice.

MY LIFE IN THE 50 STATES

If you have never seen what Williams Arena looks like, go google it quickly. It is not like a typical basketball court. This court is raised. It is interesting to see in person and always interesting to watch a game played there. Vanderbilt is the only other school I know of in the country that has a similar court, and their benches are on the baseline instead of the sidelines.

Watching the first full practice of the season is always interesting, no matter which program. I knew it wouldn't be perfect or as intense as a late season practice, but I still enjoyed it. As soon as practice was over, I jumped in my car and headed west to North Dakota. I didn't spend much time there and I don't have a juicy or interesting story of what happened while I was there. This is why I want to go back and explore more of the state. And perhaps I will visit one of the more than 10,000 lakes Minnesota has to offer when it is warmer.

MISSISSIPPI
May 1997

AT THE END OF MY freshman year of college, my suitemate, Natalie, and I headed east to make the trip home for the summer. We had already stopped in Kenedy to stay with my grandmother for a few days and wanted to drive straight to Montgomery, Alabama, where she is from. It is a 12-hour drive, but with two young college students we knew we could make it. We had a brief stop in Lake Charles, Louisiana, to have an early lunch with my aunt Cathryn. Our next stop was supposed to be Montgomery. Mother Nature had other ideas.

At the Louisiana/Mississippi border, we drove into a massive thunderstorm. It started out as a typical summer storm with some thunder and steady rain. As we kept driving, the rain got so heavy we couldn't see five feet in front of us. My car was a 1996 Ford Aspire. If you have never heard of it, I am not surprised. Even though I loved that car, and it got me everywhere I needed to go, it aspired to be a real car. It was not meant for high speeds, let alone a horrendous thunderstorm. We eventually pulled over under an overpass to see if we could wait out the rain. Now this is in 1997, a couple of years before I would have a cell phone, and several years

MISSISSIPPI

before we had heard of GPS. I did have a map, but the rain was so heavy, I couldn't see any of the road signs to see where we were. All I knew was that we had crossed into Mississippi.

After a discussion of what to do, we both decided we didn't want to drive any further in this rain. We didn't know how big the storm was, so we didn't know how long it could take us to get to Montgomery. Natalie and I agreed that we would stop at the next hotel and get a room for the night.

Thankfully, the rain let up just enough for us to drive about ten minutes further down the interstate, and we found a motel. An old motel. I'm usually not picky when it comes to hotels, but this was one that even I was nervous about stopping to stay. We didn't have much of a choice. It was late, and we did not know if the rain would come down like it had earlier. We reluctantly walked into the lobby, and a man came to the counter. His eyes moved back and forth looking at Natalie and me and asked how he could help us. I told him we needed a room for the night because the weather was too bad for us to keep going. As he started preparing everything for us, he asked if we were together. I answered yes, as if I would walk into a hotel off the interstate with some random stranger. Plus, I had said WE needed a room. Not I needed a room.

He collected all of the information he needed from me and told us that it might be a good idea if we left first thing in the morning. He didn't say why, he just looked back and forth between Natalie and I. Again, I was naïve as to why, but Natalie understood.

Not sure how much we really slept that night, but we both agreed to leave before 7:00 a.m. When we were walking out to the car, I asked Natalie why she thought that man told us to leave early. "Because you are white and I am black and we are in Mississippi," she said, matter-of-factly.

MISSOURI
October 2016

EVERY YEAR, TWICE A YEAR, the company I work for has their international convention; once in April, and again in October. Over 6,000 people from around the world, all on the same mission to inspire healthy living around the world, meet to learn more ways to help people live a healthier lifestyle and find financial freedom. The energy within this company is very hard to put into words. You cannot help but be inspired to live a healthier lifestyle, even if it is by making just one simple change.

In October of 2016, the conference happened to be in St Louis. This made me happy because it was within driving distance. I enjoy these conferences not only for the content, but also for the people I get to see. I love the fact that I have a very diverse group of friends. Within this team of people, that is exactly what we have. We have nurses, teachers, moms, single parents, stay-at-home moms, husbands and newlyweds. We have people from the city, country and some who are nomads. The best part is we are all on the same mission.

I headed to St. Louis on a Wednesday to meet up with these amazing people. Since we always have a large group, we rented

MISSOURI

an Airbnb to make it more cost efficient for everyone. I like doing this mainly so I have access to a refrigerator. I love to make my smoothies in the mornings, therefore I need a refrigerator to store my frozen fruit & other ingredients.

This convention was a special one for me. The previous year I decided to take a timeout from coaching women's basketball, which I had done for 14 years. I was unsure of what I was going to do, but my good friend, Ali Schnieder, (who is also the wife of my former head coach Brandon Schneider) talked to me about joining the business. I said sure why not!

If it allows me to earn some money and travel when I want, let's give it a go. I had been taking Juice Plus+® for five years by the time I decided to stop coaching. I knew the benefits of whole food concentrates in a capsule and what they could do for so many people. I unapologetically shared with everyone what these fruits and vegetables did for me. Because of that, I earned the promotion to sales coordinator. This meant I was supposed to walk the stage in front of everyone at the next international conference. St. Louis happened to be the conference I was walking the stage in front of over 6,000 people!

Thursday morning we had some business training before the main conference began. Since I am also a certified health coach, I met up with several other health coaches at a breakout session.

That evening, one of my friends, Casey Finnell, who I worked with at SFA, came to our Airbnb to hang out with AJ Majors and me. AJ is another dear friend I met in Nacgodoches while working at SFA. Her husband, Andy, was another assistant coach with me for the Ladyjacks. AJ also worked in the athletic department as an academic counselor. Casey worked in academics alongside AJ

MY LIFE IN THE 50 STATES

at SFA and had moved on to Lindenwood University in St Louis. Another benefit to traveling is seeing long-time friends!

Friday morning, I was second guessing crossing the stage. I honestly did not feel like it was that big of a deal to cross the stage. Yes, it is a special moment to reach the promotion; I just didn't want to walk in front of all those people.

When I was coaching, I hated having to walk into a gym in front of 50 coaches sitting along the baseline watching the games. I am quite talented when it comes to tripping on a flat surface. Thinking about walking across the stage was giving me the same anxiety. In my mind, I had decided I wasn't going to do it. I was ok with not doing it. That was until Justin and Lisa England turned to me and expressed how excited they were for me to walk across the stage. How could I not walk after seeing the pure excitement and joy their faces displayed?

When it was time for the sales coordinators to make our way to the stage, I was still nervous about tripping. Then, come to find out, we had to speak into the microphone and say our name, where we were from and what team we were on. I couldn't do anything but laugh to myself. If I messed up, oh well! I'd never see 99% of those people ever again! Gracefully, I made my way across the stage and spoke into the microphone with no stutters or trips. Mission accomplished.

Walking the stage was a great accomplishment. What filled my heart even more was to see and hear everyone who was cheering for me. The group of people who rushed to the front of the stage to watch a small town girl from south Texas receive her promotion will always have a special place in my heart. Being around that type of energy is motivation to keep going and keep doing better.

MONTANA
August 2016

My cousin, Keely, and I *volunteered* to help her uncle Larry move from Watson Lake, Yukon, in Canada, to our hometown of Kenedy, Texas. When I say *volunteered*, I mean my aunt Kathleen bought us a plane ticket and told us we were going because we were the only two who had a passport, who didn't have a schedule to worry about and who had a license to drive. Honestly, I would have asked to go even if someone else was going instead. The flight is a long one, but the drive would be epic. Kenedy is an hour southeast of San Antonio. Watson Lake is 400 miles east of Juneau, Alaska. Think about that for a second. From Watson Lake to Kenedy is 3,198 miles.

My aunt Kathleen planned for Justin, Keely's brother and Kathleen's son, to fly to Billings, Montana, to help drive as well. We were going to drop Larry off in Denver, so he could fly the remainder home. Keely, Larry and I set out from Watson Lake with an RV pulling a 14-foot trailer.

Thankfully, we were able to time it right to pick up Justin in Billings with little delay. The only delay we had was me trying to maneuver and parallel park the RV and trailer in downtown

MONTANA

Billings. I am very proud to say, I was successful in doing so with no damage to the vehicles or any pedestrians.

We had not showered in two days, so that was first on my list to do once we got to the hotel. We took turns taking a shower and were out the door in less than an hour. We were ahead of schedule to get Larry to the airport in time, so we decided to make a stop at the Battle of the Little Bighorn, which was on our way and about an hour from Billings.

I didn't remember learning very much about the Battle of the Little Bighorn, except it was where General Custer had his last stand. Although I am sure the history books said it, I did not remember that General Custer actually retreated, lost this battle and was killed by the Lakota and Cheyenne tribes, whom he was fighting.

The park is very unique. Visitors are able to drive around the entire battlefield and view it just as they did back in 1876. It was awkward for us since we were in an RV pulling a 14-foot trailer, but we did it! If you have never been to a national monument or national park, it is hard to understand the power behind it. Knowing that I was standing on the same ground where so many Native Americans were fighting for their freedom, their livelihood and their culture hit me at my core. I have never understood the thought process of running someone out of their home, off of their land, especially when they were there first and were causing no harm to any of the invaders. This park was so peaceful when we were there, yet had such a violent past.

We spent several hours at this park taking in the beauty and history of it all. I learned more that day than I ever remember in any history class I took in school. Life experiences are better schooling more often than not. Even though we could have easily spent several more hours there, we still had a deadline to get Larry to the airport in Denver, so we had to hit the road. Montana was beautiful and I wouldn't mind going back to Glacier National Park.

NEVADA
May 2009

Living in California took me away from several close friends' life milestones. I wasn't able to fly back as easily to make bridal showers, baby showers or even weddings. This was very hard for me, so whenever possible, I made sure to get to the ones I could.

May is a relatively slow month in the college basketball world. Sometimes we would have official visits, but for the most part, it is a quiet month. One of my good friends, Tana (Pyle) Drennan, was getting married in June and I already knew I would miss the wedding. This was really hard for me because we didn't have anything planned for that weekend work-wise, but if I would have scheduled to fly to Texas for the wedding, something would have come up at work and I would have been expected to cancel my trip to Texas.

The good news came when Tana's friends and fiancé decided to surprise her with a bachelorette trip to Las Vegas. This was perfect!! Vegas is a short-hour flight from San Jose, and I just knew I could make it! Except it was the weekend before I was flying to Costa Rica for vacation. And then we, as a staff, decided to bring

NEVADA

in a recruit that weekend. I couldn't commit to the Vegas trip, so I told Tana I wasn't able to make it.

Our recruiting trip was finalized about 10 days before it was going to happen, and we were not bringing the recruit in until Monday. I was going to be gone for that and felt the guilt of leaving; only partly because I did clear it with my head coach before I booked my trip to Costa Rica. However, this meant I could make the trip to Las Vegas.

I really wanted to see Tana and the rest of our friends in Vegas, especially since I would not be at the wedding. I started to research flights and found one for less than $200. I could get to Vegas Saturday morning in time for the pool and fly out first thing Sunday morning. That way, if anything random or crazy happened, I had all day to be able to get back to San Jose. DONE!! BOOKED!!

I love surprises and love surprising people, so I called one of our friends, Dawn Stuckey, to tell her that I was flying in on Saturday morning, but having to fly out first thing Sunday morning. She was excited that I was going to make it and even more excited about the surprise.

That Saturday morning, I headed to the airport in time for my flight only to find the line wrapped outside the building. The San Jose airport was doing some renovations, and this reduced the number of security lines. I didn't have a bag to check, since I was only traveling for 20 hours. I wore my swimsuit on the plane, and only packed my toothbrush, something to sleep in and something to wear out that night. I asked Dawn if I could use any of their necessities, if needed, so less for me to pack.

When I got in line for security, I had an hour before my flight. It was moving slower than a snail's pace. When I had been in line

MY LIFE IN THE 50 STATES

for 30 minutes already, and I still didn't see the metal detectors, I started to panic. I couldn't stand still, and a man in line asked if I was ok. I told him the brief story and how I couldn't afford to miss the flight because it would take away time from my friends. He allowed me to cut in front of him. Then I asked the next person if I could go, pleading my case. I was shocked that no one told me no. And within 10 minutes I was throwing my bag through the screener, along with my shoes and hat. I ran through the metal detector, grabbed my stuff and made it to the gate with several minutes to spare. Based on my experience at the airport, these next 20 hours were going to be epic.

This was before Uber existed, so I grabbed a taxi from the airport to the Imperial Palace where everyone was staying. I made sure to have Dawn S. keep Tana in the room until I got there. Dawn S. had to send the other Dawn, Dawn Andrews, down to get me, since I needed a key to get in the elevator. Dawn S. was going to make sure Tana opened the door when I knocked.

As I am knocking, I hear Dawn S. trying to get her to answer the door, and typical Tana, she didn't understand why it had to be her. I was also holding my finger over the peephole and I heard her say, "Who the hell is this and why do they have their finger over the peephole?" She cracks open the door cautiously and finally sees that it's me. Surprise worked! She couldn't believe I was there, and I was so excited to see everyone.

It was time to hit the pool and the bar. We are in Vegas, right? Since I was already in my suit, a few of the other girls and I headed downstairs to snag some chairs at the pool. Once everyone else got dressed, they met us there. Since it was May in Vegas, the pool was already packed, and we could only grab a few chairs. It was enough to throw our stuff on.

95

NEVADA

First up were drinks. The bar was having a special on Foster's beer. I am not a beer drinker, so I stuck to my usual at that time of Bacardi Light Rum and Diet Coke. It was so hot that we all drank more than we probably should have. The next round was on Dawn S. and she was bringing several of us drinks.

As she was walking back towards us, she yelled to get our attention. Just as we were turning around, all we saw were her feet slip out from underneath her, her hands went straight in the air and she fell smack on the pavement. We all burst out laughing because she did what we all would have expected any of us to do—she saved the drinks!

Never mind she was going to have a ginormous bruise on her leg, she saved the drinks! The rest of the afternoon included many more trips to the bar and many more laughs. Thankfully, no one else fell quite like Dawn did.

Next up, we had reservations at Toby Keith's restaurant called I Love This Bar and Grill, in Harrah's Casino. Eight women getting ready to go out for the evening is a task on any regular day, but after all eight have been drinking at the pool is even more comical. We managed to do it in record time and headed downstairs.

We were a typical bachelorette party having color-coordinated outfits for the night. Tana was in a white top and the rest of us in pink tops. While at the pool we didn't eat quite like we should have, so dinner was more of a grub fest. Tana didn't eat much, and we knew this was a recipe for disaster at some point later in the night.

After dinner, we made our way to the Hard Rock Hotel where they had an outdoor patio and some live music. We were able to snag a table on the patio and catch our breath. We knew we would be heading to the Playboy Club at the top of the Palms Hotel to

MY LIFE IN THE 50 STATES

dance the night away. We needed a breather if we were going to make it. Tana didn't sit down much, mostly dancing around the outdoor lamps that were there. She made her way over to one of the lamps that no one was around and casually sat down, leaned over and well, I'm sure you know the rest of that. Just as casually as she sat down, she stood up, and rallied for the rest of the night! We decided it was time to head over to the Palms before we had to answer any questions.

The Playboy Club wasn't as risqué as one might think. It was a normal club with just the name. And it was packed! We got squished between some people and drinks spilled on us, but we did not care. Our group loves to dance, and we did just that. And we did that until about 3:00 a.m. My flight was at 7:00 a.m., so I didn't have much time.

Once we got back to the hotel, I showered and changed into the clothes I was going to travel in. I was trying to take a short nap, but I was too paranoid about oversleeping. I eventually got out of bed and headed to the airport. It was a whirlwind of about 20 hours, but it was absolutely worth it, and I would do it all over again in a heartbeat.

NEBRASKA
June 2018

THE ARKANSAS RAZORBACKS baseball team was having a stellar season and made it to the College World Series. Darcheita and I had said that we would like to go to Omaha if they made the championship. Something you should know about me is that I have always wanted to go to the College World Series. I cannot tell you why. Maybe it is just the atmosphere of college athletics. I don't know, because here is something else you should know about me: I am NOT a fan of baseball. It takes too long and there is not enough action for me. It is hard for me to sit still and watch a game. However, the College World Series was a serious bucket list item for me.

The Razorbacks were playing great and did not lose a game in the tournament. They made the championship! Darcheita and I just needed to figure out which game to go to. Yvonne, the youngest Anderson, was back in the country from playing basketball overseas and was flying into Arkansas from Vegas on Tuesday morning, the day of the first game. I volunteer at the Northwest Arkansas Women's Shelter on Wednesdays, so I knew I couldn't go on Wednesday. That meant if we wanted to guarantee a game

NEBRASKA

to attend, we needed to go that day. I called Darcheita to tell her what I realized. It was 10:30 a.m. and she had just picked up Yvonne from the airport. They had just been discussing the same thing. We decided that if we were going to do it, we needed to hop in the car by noon to get there in time for the first pitch.

Before we knew it, we were on the road. Yvonne was able to shower, change quickly and arrange for the tickets to be at will-call. I gassed up my car. Darcheita made sure her four children were taken care of for the afternoon. It was summertime, so they enjoyed the day over at their Mimi and Popi's to swim and watch TV.

The drive from Fayetteville to Omaha is not a short one. It is between six and seven hours. We were cutting it close for the first pitch and were able to make it in about six hours. The traffic angels looked out for us for sure!

TD Ameritrade Park, where the series is played, is three blocks off an exit from the interstate. We were able to find some parking about a block from the interstate. This would be helpful for us when it came time to leave.

The streets were full of Arkansas and Oregon State fans. Yvonne found her way to the will-call window where our tickets would be waiting for us. As we walked in, we heard the introductions of the starters being made. It could not have been better timing. We found our way up to the concourse level and our first order of business was to find food. We didn't stop to eat before we got to the game and barely had time to eat lunch before we left Fayetteville. We each found our own desired taste for dinner and made our way to our seats.

Since we decided so late to go to the game, we didn't expect our tickets to be too close. In fact, they were at the top of the

MY LIFE IN THE 50 STATES

bleachers along the first base line. This gave us a panoramic view of the entire stadium. In my opinion, these seats were great!

The game was exciting, even for baseball. Arkansas was down 1–0 going into the fifth inning and then the runs started pouring in. We went up 4–1 and that is the way it stayed. Oregon State made a few pushes to get in some runs, but our defense was solid, and we held on to that lead. This Hog fan had never cheered so much for a baseball game, EVER!

Once the game was over, we made a beeline to the car. Again, the traffic angels looked out for us because we did not have any issues when we were trying to get out of the stadium parking lot. The first gas station we found, we stopped and filled up, grabbed some snacks and caffeine and hit the road. It was about 10:45 p.m. I started out driving and tried to get as far as I could, making it about two hours south. I still had to volunteer the next day, so I handed over the wheel to Yvonne. I was able to get several hours of sleep before she needed a break. With about an hour and a half left, I jumped in the driver's seat to bring us home.

At 5:30 a.m., I pulled into Coach A and Marcheita's house, where Yvonne was staying for the summer. I dropped those two off and made my way home. Going to the College World Series definitely lived up to the hype, and I am so glad we made that road trip. Those spontaneous trips have been some of my favorites.

NEW HAMPSHIRE
August 2016

I WAS MAKING MY WAY from Portland, Maine, to Cape Cod, Massachusetts, on my New England road trip when I stopped in Portsmouth, New Hampshire, for lunch. I wasn't going to do much but walk around, window shop and have some lunch. I made a decision to not look up what exactly I could do in Portsmouth before I got there. I decided to just go with the flow. I made my way downtown, found a parking deck and started walking.

The downtown area had an old New England-style feel to it. It was filled with local shops, diners and restaurants. My main mission was to find a keychain from the state of New Hampshire to add to my collection. I spent about 30 minutes walking around and found a local spot to eat. After enjoying lunch, I made my way to Hampton Beach State Park. I didn't find a keychain in town, so I was hoping I could find one at a tourist spot.

It was mid-August and the beach was packed. Once I found a parking spot, I made my way to the beach. My parking spot wasn't exactly legal, so I didn't have much time. I made my way across to the beach to walk around and take a few pictures. The sand was different here. It was very coarse and very hot. It was almost 90

NEW HAMPSHIRE

degrees that day, which is about 10 degrees hotter than average for that area of the country. I took my pictures and went back to my car. The sand was burning my feet in my sandals.

Several tourist shops were on the main street, but the parking was absolutely horrible to get into one of these stores. I was not about to pay $10 to go inside a store for less than five minutes.

After some searching and debating, I decided to park illegally in an unmarked parking spot with a big "TOW AWAY" sign. I took my chances and ran inside. Again, no luck. I had to leave New Hampshire without a key chain from the state. I took this as a sign that I need to go back.

NEW JERSEY
February 2017

I BELIEVE THAT PEOPLE SHOULD always strive to make themselves better and be surrounded with positive energy. AJ had introduced me to a seminar called I.M.A.G.E. It is very hard to explain what exactly it is. It is one of those things you just need to experience for yourself.

These seminars occur all over the country. When looking at the schedule, I found one in Princeton, New Jersey. This is a short drive from Philadelphia, where my friend Megan and her boyfriend at the time, Joe, lived.

I looked at my calendar to see if the timing would work for me to attend this seminar and be able to visit Megan and Joe. Timing couldn't have been better! Megan was going to be able to take the day off and go with me to the seminar. I remembered that a former player I had recruited in California, Meghin Williams, was the director of basketball operations for Princeton women's basketball. After reviewing their schedule, they happened to be playing at home against Harvard that same night. Of course, we were going to squeeze basketball into the trip if we could!

When I flew in that Friday morning, Joe was flying in from a

NEW JERSEY

work trip at the same time. He and I were able to meet up and head to the house together. Unfortunately, Megan had to work that day, which left Joe and I hanging out together. This was a bit awkward because I was still weary of Joe, like many good friends would be. (We women can be protective of our girlfriends when a new man enters the picture.)

As Megan left for work, I could tell she was a bit nervous, but I assured her it would be ok. Joe had to take care of some work in his home office, and I was about to crash, since I had been up so early for my flight.

That afternoon, Joe and I were watching TV downstairs while eating dinner and started to do what many people do to calm their nerves in awkward moments. We poured ourselves a drink. We had no idea that we both liked Bacardi. After that, I knew he couldn't be too bad of a person. By the time Megan got home, Joe and I were laughing and joking around like we were old friends. I'm sure it had nothing to do with the half of bottle of Bacardi we just drank either.

Saturday morning was early for us as we headed to New Jersey for the seminar. I knew no one at this seminar, but the good thing is, it didn't even matter. Everyone in that community is welcoming. After the seminar, we headed straight for campus for the game. Navigating around Princeton's campus at night wasn't the easiest thing for us to do. We may have taken a few wrong turns or went down a one-way, but no one was injured.

We arrived at the game a few minutes after tip off. The gym was packed. It was a rivalry game and also the alumni game. Many of the past players from Princeton were there to reunite with their teammates and cheer on the Tigers.

It was a very dramatic game as it went into overtime. After a

MY LIFE IN THE 50 STATES

hard-fought 45 minutes, Princeton came out on top, which gave everyone even more reason to celebrate. With all of the post-game festivities, I was only able to talk to Meghin for a few minutes. It was long enough to snap a photo. Even though I didn't coach Meghin, she and I still stayed in contact all those years. One thing I always appreciate about basketball has been the opportunity to create meaningful relationships with amazing people and I do my best to keep those relationships as time goes on.

NEW MEXICO
December 1995

My older brother Scott moved to Albuquerque when he was stationed at Kirtland Air Force Base. Once he got out of the Air Force, he opted to stay in Albuquerque and work as a civilian contractor for the base. I have no idea what exactly my brother did for work there. Not because I did not care, but because he couldn't tell us. I was, however, able to visit him on a few different occasions. Once, on spring break while I was in junior college and another when my mom and I made an overnight stop as we were driving my moving truck to California.

The first time, I was a senior in high school in Kenedy. My mom, grandmother and I drove from Kenedy to Albuquerque for Christmas. My dad was working in North Carolina at the time, so he flew in to meet us there. This drive was a memorable one for me. Not only was it very long, but it was also only the third time in my life I had seen snow. In fact, it snowed on us so hard on the way there that it looked like we were in a Star Wars movie and we were moving at light speed because of the way the snow was coming at us.

I am not sure how long we spent in Albuquerque, but one of the

NEW MEXICO

days we took a drive up to the Sandia Crest. The Sandia Crest is the tallest point in the Sandia Mountains outside of Albuquerque. In order to get to the top, one must take a very winding road. When I found out we were headed up the mountain for the day, I was not looking forward to it. I get motion sick as a passenger driving around town sometimes. This road was not going to be my friend at all.

In my mind, the road to the peak was never ending. It is slightly over thirteen miles from the bottom to the top, but it felt more like thirty to me. There were many hairpin turns to go along with the climb in elevation. My head was spinning like I was on the Tea Cup ride at Disneyland. Once we got to the top, we had reached an elevation of 10,678 feet. I got a quick lesson in elevation as I didn't realize how much of a difference it could make in your breathing. Factor in the dizziness from the drive and I was not the most stable person in the group. That is including my grandmother.

Once we arrived at Sandia Crest, I walked to the edge of the crest and looked out on the city of Albuquerque. The city stretched across the valley and was a beautiful sight. Although the city has half a million people, seeing it from the viewpoint really put it into perspective how large it really is. I watched my grandmother walk to the edge to take in the view. This is a picture etched in my memory, her petite body standing at the rail, bundled up in her thick blue jacket. Like me, she wasn't a fan of cold weather. Although it was another sixteen years before my grandmother passed away, this is the last trip I remember her being very able bodied and could move around without much of a struggle. I was the one struggling that day. Damn hairpin turns.

NEW YORK
December 2015

BRITNEY CLARKE WAS A FRIEND of mine from my time coaching at Stephen F. Austin. She worked in the athletic department for our academic center for athletes. She was originally from New York and eventually moved back to her home state to work at Syracuse University.

I do my best to stay in touch with my friends as much as I can. I have always done this since my time as a kid writing to friends from summer camp. I randomly texted Britney one evening to see how she was enjoying being back so close to home.

During the conversation, the topic of me coming to New York came up, because up to that point, I had never been to New York. She suggested a few good dates during the year that would be a good time to come up. The first thing that caught my attention was the St. John's vs. Syracuse game that was going to be played at Madison Square Garden. Are you kidding me? A chance to watch two storied men's basketball programs play in the world's most famous arena? HECK YES!!! Sign me up!

After some going back and forth, Britney was able to get it squared away with her schedule so that we could make this

NEW YORK

happen. For those of you who do not work in college athletics, you have to understand that plans can be changed last minute due to recruiting or any other random circumstances with college athletes. Being able to monitor and adjust plans when needed is key. I knew going into this trip that something might come up for her and plans might alter or be cancelled altogether. I did not care.

On a Thursday, I flew into Syracuse where Britney lived. I was exhausted because the day before, Megan and I had driven from Fort Worth back to Fayetteville after a game at TCU watching our friend, Angela, coach against SFA, where I had previously coached. Britney was able to pick me up after work and we headed downtown to eat. She took me to a local spot that was very eclectic and unique to the city. It is always great to catch up with friends and see where life has taken them since your paths had previously crossed.

The following day, Britney had to work that morning and I caught up on my sleep. Since I had started my Juice Plus+® business, I was able to do this from home or anywhere else I traveled to. I took the morning to sleep in, walk around the neighborhood and work on my business. My legs get very restless after flying, so it was good to get them moving.

Britney came to get me at lunchtime to take a tour of the athletic facilities. I appreciate being able to see what other schools have to offer student athletes in regards to their practice facilities, academic services and weight room. I was also able to catch up with the head women's basketball coach, Quentin Hillsman. I have known Quentin for several years, dating back to when I was coaching at Tyler Junior College. Friday evening, we hit the downtown area again for some food and drinks. We were leaving for the city the next day, which led to a short night out.

MY LIFE IN THE 50 STATES

As I stated before, life in athletics can throw curve balls at you. Originally, we had planned to go to the city on Friday, but Britney had a last-minute football obligation Saturday morning. Monitor and adjust was always my motto while I was coaching, and I still live by that today. It wasn't a problem to just leave later in the day. I went with Britney to the office and waited while she talked to a few football recruits. We were on the road by noon.

Driving from Syracuse to New York City was not the drive I was expecting. It took us through some rolling hills/mountains that reminded me of Arkansas. I did my best to stay awake through the drive. If I am sitting in the passenger seat, I usually fall asleep within the first hour. I credit this to my mom who, when I was a child, would plan our road trips during my and my brother's nap times. The road seems to soothe me.

We got down to Britney's parents' house, dropped off our bags and headed to the city. Since our day was cut short, we were going to have to speed through some of the sights of New York City.

There were a few things that were a must see for me: Times Square, the Rockefeller Center Christmas Tree, the Today Show Plaza and One World Trade Center. Of course it would have been great to see the Statue of Liberty, taken the Staten Island Ferry, crossed the Brooklyn Bridge and walked through Central Park among a list of other things, but we were short on time and I would take what I could get.

Britney parked the car in one of the neighborhoods that she remembered as a kid, and we took the subway into the city. Our first stop was dinner in Times Square. We were able to find a TGI Friday's, but the wait was almost two hours. After we debated for a few minutes, a couple left the bar area and we sprinted to take those seats. The long wait was avoided.

113

NEW YORK

Dinner was nothing to rave about, except that it was in Times Square. That was special enough. After dinner we ventured out into the hustle and bustle of Times Square. I never felt more like a country kid out of place as I did in the heart of New York City. Again, my life was feeling like a movie. I wanted to stand in the middle of Times Square, stretch out my arms and twirl around. I decided to save that for the next trip.

Christmas time brings thousands of people to Rockefeller Center to see the iconic Christmas tree lit up and to skate in the skating rink. The streets had been closed off because there were so many people trying to make their way there. It reminded me of a crowd after a football game trying to exit the stadium. I am a determined person, so I grabbed Britney's hand and we weaved our way through the crowds to be able to see the tree. I grabbed a few pictures there in front of the Today Show windows, and we continued on.

We decided to make our way to One World Trade Center on foot. Doing this allowed us to see more of the city and a few more landmarks. We passed the New York City Library. Someone was having a wedding reception that evening. It never crossed my mind to have a reception at a library, but from the looks of the outside and how they had pictures lined up, it looked very elegant.

As we were walking toward the Empire State building, Britney and I chatted casually, stopping in a few of the tourist shops to pick up my key chains and a few other souvenirs.

When we came to an intersection where we had to stop at the stoplight, I noticed a man in front of me had a picture of someone with red pants and a cream colored sweater on. I thought to myself, *that's exactly what I am wearing.* Then I looked closer and realized it WAS me...from behind! The light turned green for

MY LIFE IN THE 50 STATES

us to walk and I whispered to Britney what I just saw. I couldn't believe it, and neither could she. We walked fast to try and keep up with the guy and see if he would pull it up again on his phone.

At the next stoplight, he still had it pulled up. I wanted to say something to him, but was unsure of exactly what I should say. What if I was mistaken and it really wasn't me? It was me though! Or was it? I didn't want to cause an unnecessary scene, so we just kept following the man.

After three blocks, he noticed we were right on his tail. He glanced over his shoulder a time or two to see if we were still following. I decided to mess with his head. A friend of mine in Arkansas, Jessah, who happened to be from New York, was training in Ju Jitsu at the time. We recently had a conversation about her upcoming fight. I started to have the same conversation with Britney as if it were me who was fighting. The man's pace picked up and so did ours. After I answered Britney's question of what my record was (I said I was 17–0 with 15 KOs), he took a sharp right. She and I laughed the remainder of our walk.

We made it to One World Trade Center about 30 minutes before it closed for the evening. We were still allowed to go in the memorial, but I couldn't do it. I do not know anyone personally who died in that attack, but as an American, I felt it to my core. When we walked up to the 9/11 memorial pools, I was almost paralyzed. Thinking of all the tragedy that occurred there made me lose my breath. There are honestly no words that can accurately describe what it is like to visit that memorial. I know I have said this before, but you really have to visit to understand what it is like.

I was very emotional as I walked around the pools. The names of every person who died in the 2001 and 1993 attacks are inscribed

115

NEW YORK

into bronze panels edging the memorial pools. As I continued walking, I noticed that every so often there would be a rose placed on top of a name. Seeing those flowers purposely placed sent another wave of emotions through me. I wanted to take pictures of myself in front of the pools, but it did not seem like the right thing to do. How could I smile in front of a memorial commemorating such a tragic event? This is the most tragic, impactful world event that has happened in my lifetime. I took pictures of the pools as they were lit up with the water running over the side. I hope the next time I visit New York I am able to emotionally handle visiting the inside of the museum.

It was getting late, so Britney and I made our way back to the subway, took it to where she had parked the car and headed home. Sunday morning, I woke up to the smell of breakfast being made. Britney's dad was up cooking for us before we headed back to the city for the game. Britney told her dad about our adventure stalking the man who we think took my picture. Her dad was a cop and said very definitively, "Oh yeah, he took a picture of you. No doubt."

It was getting time for us to hit the road and head into town. We did the same as the night before, parking and taking the subway to Madison Square Garden. Like many other basketball arenas, they share the arena with their hockey team, the New York Rangers. In order to keep the ice frozen, the temperatures are kept low. I was freezing the entire game.

I was excited to see this game, not only because of the storied rivalry, but also it had two well-known coaches. Jim Boeheim coaches the Orangemen of Syracuse and Chris Mullen was coaching St. John's at the time. Unfortunately, Jim Boeheim was suspended the first nine games of that season by the NCAA for some recruiting violations over a long period of time. This game

116

MY LIFE IN THE 50 STATES

happened to be during his suspension. It played into St. John's favor, as they won 84–72.

Since my flight was early the next morning and she had to work, we hit the road immediately after the game. Well, after I snapped a few pictures of myself under the Madison Square Garden sign.

I definitely was not a good riding partner, as I fell asleep on the way home. I struggled to keep my head from bobbing, but the sleep won. I felt so bad that I fell asleep while Britney drove us home. She was an awesome host, and I will forever be grateful for my first trip to New York.

NORTH CAROLINA

May 1997

I HAD SOME AMAZING EXPERIENCES in the state of North Carolina. I went to my first ever concert, which happened to be Tina Turner. My dad worked for Sara Lee and she was doing a special concert for all their employees. I was able to get tickets to the Wake Forest vs. Duke men's basketball game. Getting to see my best friend, Gigi (Miller) Johnson, compete at the NCAA Outdoor National Track Championships in Durham was special. She placed second in the heptathlon. Yes, she was a beast. But the one thing that had the biggest impact on my life almost didn't happen.

After that long road trip with my suitemate, Natalie, I had to keep going to Winston-Salem, North Carolina, where my parents lived. Technically they lived in Rural Hall, which is a small community just north of the city. I had an eight-hour drive from Montgomery, and for some reason, I didn't leave Alabama until late. This meant I was getting to my parent's house late.

My dad worked for Sara Lee, and as they did for the Olympics, which I detailed in Georgia, they were sponsors for The Crosby. The Crosby was a huge celebrity golf tournament that was started

NORTH CAROLINA

by Bing Crosby and continued on by his widow, Katherine Crosby. All of the big names in sports and entertainment were at this tournament.

My parents were volunteering, and my dad had a pass for me to watch all the celebrities roll through. The only catch... I had to wake up and leave with them at 4:00 a.m. I am not a morning person AT ALL! I debated the entire drive home from Alabama if I was still going to go. My mom came into my room at about 3:15 a.m. to wake me up and I told her I didn't want to go. She really had no idea what she was saying when she told me, "If you don't go, you are going to regret it."

I managed to get myself showered, teeth brushed and out the door with them. My plan was to sit at the first tee and just watch everyone tee off. I did this for the first couple of groups, one that included Julius Erving, or Dr. J, as everyone in the basketball world knows him. The third group pulled up and there was a man who looked very familiar to me, but between how early it was and how little sleep I had, I couldn't figure it out. He pulled up to where I was standing, said hello and remarked how surprising it was to see people out that early. I was polite, smiled and agreed that is was really early to be out there, but it was worth it.

I was racking my brain as to who this man was. He reminded me of my maternal grandfather with his stature and slight limp. I knew once they announced his name when he teed off, I would feel like an idiot for not realizing it.

The announcer started to list off all of the accomplishments of this man. He played for Hall of Fame coach Don Haskins at UTEP. His is the only coach to win a NJCAA, NIT and NCAA title. He led the 1994 Arkansas Razorbacks to their only men's basketball national championship. He is Nolan Richardson. I face palmed

120

MY LIFE IN THE 50 STATES

my forehead and laughed at myself. How did I not recognize Nolan Richardson? I blamed it on the lack of sleep and how early it was.

After Coach Richardson teed off, I waited to get his autograph. For some odd reason, I decided to blurt out that I had played my freshman year at a junior college in Texas. He looked up from signing my autograph with disbelief and asked me where I played. I told him Odessa College. He chuckled a bit and told me he started his college coaching career at Western Texas, which was in the same conference as Odessa. We both laughed, he thanked everyone there who came out and the group he was with moved on.

As I said before, my plan was to stay and watch everyone tee off. Another group passed and I was already bored. I decided I was going to catch up to Coach Richardson and walk with his group for a few holes. I searched out the concession trailer where my parents were working to let them know I would be walking around.

I found the group that Coach was walking with, but didn't say anything. I didn't want him to think I was following him, although that is exactly what I was doing. He spotted me pretty quickly and struck up conversation. I only intended to walk a couple of holes with them. We started talking. Well, he started asking me all kinds of questions and I answered. He asked me everything about my family, where I was from, what I planned to do in college, after college.

At the time, I was planning to go to Southwest Texas (now known as Texas State) in San Marcos. He told me stories about opening up the Chaparral Center on the campus of Midland College and traveling around the conference we played in.

Before I realized it, I had walked all 18 holes with him. Right

NORTH CAROLINA

before he went back into the clubhouse, Coach gave me a big hug and told me to let him know what I ended up doing after Odessa. He may not have meant it, but I took it to heart.

Later that evening, I told my parents about my time with Coach Richardson. My dad suggested to me that I write him to see if he could help me somehow become an athletic trainer at Arkansas. Not too sure how serious my dad was about this either, but again, I took it to heart. I wrote a letter to Coach to see if he could talk with the head trainer at Arkansas and I could somehow get in. And when I say write, I mean snail mail. Email was fairly new, and I was still used to sending handwritten letters.

After a couple of months, I still didn't get a response. I am not sure exactly what type of response I thought I was going to get. I ended up looking up the phone number to the basketball office, held my breath and dialed the number.

Another thing most people cannot believe about me is that I despise having to call someone that I do not know. Terry Mercer, the secretary at the time and still to this day, answered the phone and first told me that Coach was going into a meeting. Now I know that is an easy excuse for deterring random phone calls from anyone claiming to have met a Hall of Fame coach at a golf tournament in North Carolina three months prior.

After a short hold, Coach Richardson got on the phone and we exchanged pleasantries. He knew I was calling in regard to the letter I sent him. He promised he would pass along my name to Dave England, the long-time athletic trainer for men's basketball at the University of Arkansas. I honestly had no idea how this phone call was going to go, but by the time it was all said and done, I was to be expecting a phone call from Dave in the near future.

MY LIFE IN THE 50 STATES

Two weeks later, I received that phone call and Dave was able to offer me a small amount of money as a scholarship. I was ecstatic! I told my parents just knowing they were going be as excited as I was and say yes.

Since I had graduated from a Texas high school and my dad paid taxes in North Carolina, I had two states I could choose to go to college. Then I pulled Arkansas out of a hat.

My dad said it would be tough, gave me a short lecture that I don't remember any of except that if I could find X amount more dollars, they would try to make it work. I found X amount more dollars and off I was to attend the University of Arkansas. My experience there shaped me into the coach and person I am today. And to think, I wanted to sleep in that morning. Thank goodness I listened to my mom.

NORTH DAKOTA
September 2017

REMEMBER THAT FOUR STATE ROAD trip I planned? Well, after leaving Minneapolis, I headed to Jamestown, North Dakota. When I planned this road trip, I searched for the top ten things to do in each state. I honestly knew very little about any of the four states I was traveling to. The Internet helped me decide what I was going to see.

I found more things than I thought I would want to see in North Dakota, but I had to factor in time and driving distance. I needed to stick to attractions along I-94. One thing that caught my attention was the world's largest buffalo and a white buffalo.

Both of these were at the Buffalo Museum in Jamestown. The world's largest buffalo towers at 26 feet tall and weighs a hefty 60 tons. This concrete sculpture was created in 1959 for the Buffalo Museum. There is also a herd of buffalo owned by the museum in the pasture that follows the interstate. In this herd is a white buffalo. White buffalo are considered sacred by the Lakota Nation. Unfortunately, Dakota Miracle was not roaming close to the museum, so I did not get a chance to see him.

I spent about an hour roaming around the museum and the

NORTH DAKOTA

grounds before hopping back in my car and continuing west. I noticed the cloud coverage start to get thicker the further west I drove. They were not threatening storm clouds; it just made the area very gloomy.

A few hours later, I came to one of the visitor's centers of the Theodore Roosevelt National Park just outside of Medora, North Dakota. This particular one overlooked parts of the Badlands. I wanted to get a closer look of the valleys and canyons. As soon as I opened the door, I was slapped in the face with some fierce, cold wind. The temperature had dropped to 38 degrees. I did NOT pack for this weather.

I took in the view of the overlook. I had read that buffalo roamed this part of the state and I was searching to see my first one. One would think that as big as they are, they would be easy to see. I wanted to find one, but the cold was making me debate with myself on if it was worth it. I decided to take one last scan over the horizon and saw the first one, and then the second and third. How did I miss this entire herd? They were just far enough that I couldn't get a good picture, but close enough that I could see them well with my own eyes. I finally saw a buffalo in the wild! I was good to go after that!

I turned to run back to my car to get out of the cold. I just about slipped and fell when I saw I was about to run through a large mound of buffalo &@#! I looked around and there were several more piles of it around the grounds of the visitor's center. I am not sure how I dodged these as I got out of my car. That could have made for a very unpleasant drive to South Dakota.

I was not able to get a picture next to the state sign at the entrance to the state. However, I decided to get a picture next to the park sign. I set my phone up against a rock I found and

126

MY LIFE IN THE 50 STATES

snapped the memory. I wanted to get on the road because I still had four and a half hours to drive to Custer, South Dakota. Thankfully, the cloud cover started to thin out and the sun peeked its head through as it was setting.

I approached the South Dakota border on a small two-lane highway and stopped at the sign to snap my picture. By the looks of it, many people do the same thing because there is a worn piece of shoulder where many cars have stopped before. I did my usual set up and as I was taking the picture, I noticed there was the sign for North Dakota. YES!!! I could get two different state pictures in a matter of feet! I contemplated running across the highway, but decided to drive over there. There was no shoulder on this road, only the two lanes and dirt.

It reminded me of the road in the movie *Forrest Gump* where he finally decides to turn around. I drove over, snapped my picture and made my way south. Always make sure you look up and around at your surroundings. You might miss something you were looking for.

OHIO
July 2011

DURING THE MONTH OF JULY, recruiting for college coaches is very hectic. There is a lot of strategic planning that goes into arranging four coaches to attend tournaments around the country in two 10-day spans. Sometimes plans change, a player may change teams, or the tournament may not be as good as expected, so coaches will change their travel plans and go to another tournament. Larger schools have the luxury of using a travel agent to make these arrangements. I was our travel agent.

I was planning to meet our head coach, Brandon Schneider, down in Orlando for a tournament. The days leading up to our meeting, we realized it wasn't as urgent as originally planned. We needed to watch other players at a different tournament. Once we made the official decision, I got to work rescheduling Brandon and my flights.

I used Southwest Airlines as much as possible because this airline makes it easiest to make changes. As I was trying to reschedule Brandon and send him to Chicago, I was getting phone calls and updates from our other assistants about the tournaments they were attending. I had to work some magic with

OHIO

the plane schedule, and I may have stressed out a little with the prices, since we were making the arrangements the day prior, but in the end, it all worked out. Brandon would head to Chicago and I would head to Cincinnati.

The next morning, I headed to the airport, checked in and was at my gate with about an hour to spare. I noticed there was a more than usual amount of kids and families at this gate. I shrugged it off and planned my schedule of games for Cincinnati. But there was something that wouldn't let me stop thinking about all the kids at this gate. I decided to look up at the gate to make sure I was at the correct gate. It said Orlando. I was definitely at the wrong gate, so I grabbed my ticket to see where I was supposed to be. It said Orlando. With all the commotion of changing Brandon's ticket and the many phone calls I made, I never changed my ticket to Cincinnati.

I wasn't too stressed until I talked to the gate agent. I asked how difficult it would be for me to go to Cincinnati instead of Orlando; apparently, very difficult because Southwest Airlines doesn't fly to Cincinnati. If I could use an emoji, the face palm one would be appropriate here. After some quick thinking, the agent was able to switch my flight to Columbus and I could make the short drive to Cincinnati. One more problem—my luggage. I had to sprint downstairs to the help desk, OUTSIDE of security, to see if they MIGHT be able to find my black roller bag that doesn't look like anyone else's and stop it from being loaded onto the Orlando flight. Thankfully, the baggage workers worked with us and found the bag just as it was about to be loaded on the flight.

Now I know I technically wasn't in Ohio when this happened, but it is still a great story of my experience with Ohio. I eventually made it to Cincinnati, Brandon made it to Chicago and we were able to see all the players we needed to see.

OKLAHOMA
December 2015

DURING MY TIME AT San Jose State, I became really close with two of my coworkers, Angela Gonzaga and Megan (Osmer) Westerfer. Our players started calling us Charlie's Angels because, well, we were three women who always managed to save the day. Of course, the players were thinking of the modern-day Charlie's Angels with Lucy Lu, Drew Barrymore and Cameron Diaz. We thought it fit, and we still to this day refer to each other as angels.

After we went our separate ways from San Jose State, Angela found her way to TCU in Fort Worth, Texas. Megan was out of coaching, as was I, and living in Philadelphia with then boyfriend, Joe. I was in Arkansas and planning to go visit Angela when they were playing Stephen F. Austin. I was looking forward to seeing not only her, but also some of my former players and fans from SFA.

I mentioned my plans to Megan about this, and she got the idea that we could surprise Angela with Megan flying down also. It was going to be a quick trip since I would have to drive back from Fort Worth after the game because I was flying out of Fayetteville to go knock-off another state from my list—New York. Megan was able to arrange her flight to fly out at the same time as mine.

OKLAHOMA

Megan and I, along with our other former coworker, Brett, were able to pull off surprising Angela for her birthday earlier that year. We were not sure if this would go as easy, but we were going to do our best! And it worked! Huge surprise to Angela that the angels made the reunion happen again!

The game had a 7:00 p.m. tip and we were on the road by 9:30 p.m. It was going to be rough, but between the two of us, and some caffeine, we knew we could pull it off. Megan and I chatted almost the entire trip.

Around 1:00 a.m., I was telling Megan about all the states I had been to and she decided to count all of her states. She rambled off about 30 states and we talked about some of the experiences we each had in the states.

After a brief pause, Megan blurted out, "Oh, and I've never been to Oklahoma." I looked at her very confused, looked around and said, "Megan, we are IN Oklahoma right now." She looked at me as serious as can be and said, "Well, guess I can cross it off now."

I HAD BEEN LIVING IN California for a little over a year when the 2008 Olympic Trials for track and field were being held in Eugene, Oregon. My best friend, Gigi (Miller) Johnson, was a heptathlete and was competing to make the USA Olympic Team. I am no stranger to long road trips, so I hopped in my little green Honda Civic and hit the road up north for an eight-hour road trip.

As it happens many times in California summers, there was a fire threatening the interstate that I was supposed to be traveling on. When I set out on the trip, the fires were far enough off the road that I was safe. I have dealt with natural disasters such as hurricanes, earthquakes and tornadoes, so I knew being prepared was going to be important. I packed some blankets, extra food and water just on the off chance something was to happen and I was stranded, I would be ok. I was secretly eager to see the fires because I had never seen one up close before, but I did know the danger that it presented.

Heading into Redding along Interstate 5, I started to see a different haze in the air. My heart rate probably doubled because I had no idea where exactly the fires were. Were they close to the

OREGON

interstate or were they still far enough off they were not a presenting danger? Because the roads were still open, I figured I was safe to continue my way up north.

I made it to Eugene just in time to catch the tail end of dinner with Gigi, her husband and coach Chris Johnson, and all the athletes from Penn State that were competing in the trials. Chris was the assistant men and women's track coach at Penn State at the time and had several current and former athletes competing during the two-week trials, as well as some competing with Gigi in the heptathlon. In other words, they are some bad asses! The heptathlon is where athletes compete in seven different events over the course of two days. These seven events are the 100m hurdles, high jump, shot put, 200m, long jump, javelin and 800m.

On the first day, the first four events happen over the course of five hours, and on the second day, the remaining three events take place in three and a half hours. Athletes score points based on their times, distance and height of the respective event, not the place they come in during the individual competition. It is a brutal event, and athletes must be physically AND mentally tough in order to compete in the heptathlon.

This was Gigi's best year. She was in the best shape she had ever been in— mentally, physically and emotionally. Because of that, I was convinced this was her year to make the Olympics.

She had always said that if I made the Final Four as a coach, she would be there for me, and I agreed that if she ever made the Olympics, I would be there for her.

I had already begun pricing tickets with miles and money to Beijing. I made sure to tell my head coach at the time that I would be flying to Beijing for about five days to watch her compete. I found a ticket that got me there the day before she competed and

134

MY LIFE IN THE 50 STATES

left the morning after she would finish. I was ready to exhaust all plane miles, get over my fear of traveling alone in a foreign country, and spend a little cash I didn't quite have in order to watch my friend fulfill her dream.

The first day is always a great one. She got second overall in the hurdles and 200m and was sitting in fourth heading into day two. She felt great after that first day and believed she was close enough to be able to edge out Diana Pickler, who was sitting in third. The long jump was going to be where she would be able to jump (no pun intended) into a qualifying spot. Things started off good with a great jump, and next came the javelin. Not exactly her best event, but again, she gets points for the distance, not the place she comes in.

Unfortunately, the one event that she hated was up last, the 800m run. The good thing is she knew she just had to come in three seconds faster than Diana Pickler and her trip to Beijing would be booked. Her mom and I were so nervous for her. The break time between the javelin and 800m was so nerve wrecking for us because we had no control over it. It was all up to her to run her best, and all we could do was yell. And jump up and down.

We started out watching the race about midway up the stands, so we could see the entire track. When the gun went off, all I could do was think about how we were going to celebrate and how I was going to tell my head coach that I would be in China for a few days.

I honestly don't remember much of her first lap, but I do remember the second. She was ahead of Diana, but I couldn't figure out by how much. It wasn't much. As she hit the 200m mark, her mom took off down the bleachers and I quickly followed. If anyone knows me, they know it was a miracle I didn't

135

OREGON

fall sprinting down the bleachers. As she came down the home stretch, I yelled as loud as I could, knowing she probably couldn't hear me. Her mom and I jumped up and down probably the last 50 meters knowing it wouldn't help her run faster, but that's all we could do.

As she crossed the finish line, we could tell she was exhausted. The one thing we couldn't tell is if she finished far enough in front of Diana, who finished right after her. Her mom and I held onto each other waiting to see the time flash on the big screen. I know it was only a matter of seconds, but it felt like forever. That sounds so cliché to say, but it is the absolute truth. When her time flashed, and the overall standings were posted, my heart sank. She finished 1.7 seconds faster, not the three seconds needed. She was going to be an alternate, yet again.

We knew she would have to do everything the athletes who qualified would do, such as get drug tested, right after the race. We decided to catch the bus back to the car and then to the hotel. I am not sure how many words Mrs. Miller and I spoke, but I remember both of us saying we just couldn't believe it.

As we were getting on the bus to the car, we see Gigi running towards the bus. She was still in her competition uniform, shoes barely on, a slew of clothes in her hands and she was balling her eyes out. We yelled at the bus driver to stop so she could get on the bus with us. This crushed me to see her like this. I honestly didn't know how to console her. Her mom just hugged her as she cried. We got back to the hotel, and I did the only thing I knew to do—told her she needed to shower and we would go get something to eat.

We found a cute little restaurant to eat not far from the hotel. Not sure of what we even ate, but I know she chowed down. After

MY LIFE IN THE 50 STATES

doing a heptathlon, her appetite was intense. I let her steer the conversation whichever way she wanted it to go. We ended up going to the grocery store, so she could get some more snacks for the remaining days she was there. I wasn't sure what the right thing to do for her that day was. I could have been way off base, and maybe I didn't do enough, but it was all that I knew to do. As we were checking out, she told me that she appreciated me getting her out of the hotel room, and it was exactly what she needed. That's all I needed.

PENNSYLVANIA
October 2015

DURING MY TIME IN CALIFORNIA, I became good friends with a woman I went to college with, Stephanie. Strangely enough, she and I ran in the same circle of friends in college, but never hung out together. Another mutual friend of ours introduced us in California, and we quickly became each other's go-to when adventuring into San Francisco or Oakland. After I moved to Texas, she moved to Philadelphia with her new husband, Chris.

The first fall I was out of coaching, I was having withdrawal from no practice, so I needed to keep busy. I gave Stephanie a call and I decided to visit her in Philadelphia on Halloween weekend. I had never been to Philadelphia, and being a tourist in a historic town sounded like a great idea to me. As I was planning this trip, I decided to call Megan, who was living on the west coast at the time. She hadn't moved out to Philadelphia with Joe quite yet, but was planning to fly in and surprise him the same weekend. What a perfect weekend!

When I got to Philadelphia, Stephanie drove me around downtown to see a few of the iconic Philadelphia landmarks; the LOVE sculpture being one, and of course, the Museum of Art's famous

PENNSYLVANIA

steps where Rocky Balboa trained in the movie *Rocky*. No one in that city can complain about not having a gym membership, because that place is the best free gym anyone could ask for!

Friday morning, Stephanie took me downtown to check out Independence National Park. This is where Independence Hall and the Liberty Bell are located. Independence Hall is where the Declaration of Independence was signed and the infamous cracked Liberty Bell hangs in the Liberty Bell Center. Seeing the Liberty Bell and thinking of all it has gone through, the years of distress and what it stood for, was fascinating.

This area is filled with museums and landmarks detailing all of the early American history that took place in this city. Something else we stumbled upon was "College Game Day." The ESPN Saturday morning show was in town for the matchup between Temple and Notre Dame football. It was fun to see the setup in person. We even took a picture on the mock set. This is one of those experiences that although I have always wanted to do it, have not actually set aside time to do, but I am glad we stumbled upon it.

That night, we were able to meet up with Megan and Joe, along with a few of his childhood friends. We met up at Del Frisco's, a steakhouse that was once First Pennsylvania Bank. This restaurant/bar is one of a kind. I am a big fan of places that have been revamped and transformed from its original purpose, but still hold historical value. The atmosphere in there was vibrant, very urban, and filled with that unique energy that only comes from life in the city. When we first arrived, the entire place was packed and buzzing. A few hours later, I may have been buzzing because I didn't notice the place had all but cleared out.

Joe's friend, Marty, (wait until West Virginia to see what these

MY LIFE IN THE 50 STATES

two did) was hungry and wanted some dessert. The kitchen had long since closed at Del Frisco's. Marty was determined to get some dessert, so he made a phone call. About ten minutes later, a young man came up the stairs to the bar where we were sitting and handed Marty a bag from the Cheesecake Factory. He had called a friend of his who sent over one of the waiters from Cheesecake Factory with several different types of cheesecake for all of us to share. We couldn't do anything but grab a fork and taste the cheesecakes.

That night, I woke up out of my sleep with a very uneasy feeling. It was about 4:00 a.m. and I couldn't shake the feeling. Something didn't feel right. I lay in bed for another 10 minutes trying to figure out what was going on and finally drifted back to sleep.

When I woke up a few hours later, I saw on Facebook that Ron Harris, the father of one of my former players, Daylyn Harris, had passed away in the middle of the night after a hard-fought battle with cancer. Not too long after I read that startling news, I received some additional news that a friend from college, DeeDee Campbell, had lost her father to cancer around the same time. Both of these young ladies cherished the relationship they had with their fathers like no other. I texted both of them immediately and sent my condolences.

The only thing else I knew to do was pray. My father was battling stage IV cancer at the same time. To this day, he continues to win his battle. I had an amazing time in Philadelphia, the city of brotherly love. I just can't help but think of both Daylyn and DeeDee when I think of Philadelphia.

RHODE ISLAND
August 2016

AS PART OF MY ROAD trip through New England, I was passing through Rhode Island on the way to Connecticut to see a Connecticut Suns game. I told part of this story in the Connecticut chapter. This is what happened to me before I reached the game.

I was driving from Cape Cod, Massachusetts, to Uncasville, Connecticut, where the Suns play. I wanted to stop in Providence, Rhode Island, along the way for lunch. I set out for a restaurant that a coaching friend of mine told me about. It was by the water, served good food and was close to the mall.

After lunch, I went to the mall and just happened to walk in on the side of a massage store. I checked my watch and the app one more time to see if I had enough time to get a massage. Since I had spent the last week in a car, I needed the massage. I was really glad to find out they could take me right away for an hour. When my massage was finished, I headed out to scout out the layout of the mall and find my favorite stores. I am a pretty quick shopper. If I don't see anything right away that catches my eye, I am out of there. I am not much of a searcher. However, when there is a 75% off sale at New York & Company and Express, I take my time.

RHODE ISLAND

I did a little bit of damage in those two stores and realized I had about an hour and a half until game time. To get to the arena would take me about 45 minutes to an hour. I jumped in my rental and thought I was making a quick getaway. WRONG! The line to get out of the garage was wrapped all the way to the fourth level, where I was located. As I inched closer to the outer edge, I noticed traffic EVERYWHERE!! I looked at my watch and realized it was 5:00 p.m. It never crossed my mind to take into consideration rush hour traffic.

I didn't want to be late to the game, but there was absolutely nothing that I could do. I impatiently waited in my car to get out of downtown Providence. Once I was able to hit the highway, I went as fast as I could. I had about 40 miles to go in 30 minutes.

Any time my GPS gives me an estimated time of arrival, I take that as a challenge to beat that time. If anyone could do it, it would be me. And I did. If you have forgotten what happened when I got there, just flip back to Connecticut.

SOUTH CAROLINA
March 2017

AT SFA, WE WON CONSECUTIVE regular season conference championships in 2014 and 2015. Unfortunately, we were upset in our conference tournament both years and were forced to go to a post-season tournament each year other than the NCAA tournament.

In 2014, we went to the Women's Basketball Invitational (WBI). We entered the tournament as a #4 seed and were able to host the first two rounds, defeating Texas State and Boise State. Next up, College of Charleston. The biggest difference between the NCAA tournament and the WBI is that teams do not get private chartered flights to their next game. We would be playing at College of Charleston and if we won, would have to fly out to either Chicago to play University of Illinois at Chicago or Fairfield, Connecticut, to play Fairfield. The one thing we knew for sure is that we needed to pack warm clothes.

Luckily, we had about a week to prepare for College of Charleston and travel wasn't going to be too difficult. We were able to leave the day before and arrive in time to get a good practice in on the court. Getting a feel for the gym is always important

SOUTH CAROLINA

for the players. The depth perception of the goal varies gym to gym and can really mess up a player's vision. Practice was a good one, especially after a day of travel. The next day, we went through our normal game day routine—our athletic trainer, Loree, and I worked out early in the morning, the team met for breakfast and we departed for shoot-around.

Afterwards, we headed back to the hotel to go over our scouting report of our opponent and to eat our pregame meal. By the time our game started, we found out that if we won, we would be heading to Chicago. UIC had beat Fairfield by 30.

We had a solid first half, going into the locker room at halftime by six points. Our girls came out strong in the second half, building our lead to 19. We got a little too comfortable and after several small runs, College of Charleston pulled within three, thanks to second chance points. Going to our star player, Porsha Roberts, at the end of the game she was fouled and was able to hit one of two free throws with three seconds left to go up four points and seal the victory. This was a record-breaking game for the Ladyjacks; it was the first in school history to win three postseason tournament games. It was quite the accomplishment, since the Ladyjack basketball program is one of the most winningest Division I basketball programs in the country. Another record that was broken occurred in the first half when Porsha Roberts blocked her first shot, passing Amy Collins. Porsha still had another year of eligibility. She finished her career with 246 blocks.

The win was great to celebrate; however, we couldn't celebrate long. UIC was scheduling our championship game for 3:00 p.m., Sunday afternoon. We had to figure out how to get 30 people to Chicago from Charleston. It was Friday night about 11:00 p.m. when our director of basketball operations was making flight

146

MY LIFE IN THE 50 STATES

reservations. We had to break up our group onto three different flights, with the first one departing at 6:00 a.m. I was on the first flight. This meant we were leaving the hotel about 4:00 a.m., less than four hours of the time we received confirmation. It was a great time in Charleston, but we were ready to play in the championship game.

As I told the story in Illinois, everyone made it to Chicago on time and with their bags. Unfortunately, the run of records for that season ended. The exhaustion of the late Friday night game with the travel caught up with us, and we lost to UIC in the championship game. It was an amazing season and I wouldn't have wanted to do it with any other staff or players.

SOUTH DAKOTA
September 2017

SOUTH DAKOTA WAS A PART of my road trip in 2017. Before I left Arkansas, I made sure to check the weather, so that I could pack appropriately. Since I was driving, I am not sure why I did not pack extra clothes. By the time I got to Minnesota, the weather had already changed and I had to go shopping at the Mall of America for some additional long sleeve shirts. What I wasn't expecting was the drastic drop in temperature when I was on my way to Custer, South Dakota.

I drove across the state of North Dakota and headed south on Highway 85. The further I drove south, the more the temperature dropped. By the time I pulled into the parking lot at my hotel in Custer, it was 28 degrees. On October 3rd. And I didn't have a jacket. Mount Rushmore was going to be interesting.

The following morning, I got dressed as warmly as I possibly could have. Thankfully, I grabbed a grey duster (a long open sweater) at my stop at the Mall of America, and it came in clutch. The morning was foggy, dreary and chilly.

I wanted to go hiking but decided against it, since I was by myself. I didn't know the trails and the wildlife seemed to scare

SOUTH DAKOTA

me more than anywhere else. I'm not sure exactly why, but at the time it did. Instead, I chose to drive Needles Highway. Our secretary at SFA, Darba Rollins, had traveled this highway a couple months prior with her husband and suggested it for me.

Needles Highway wound through Custer State Park and led me to Mount Rushmore. The narrow highway led me to some old caves, very narrow passages through the mountains and a perfectly still blue lake.

After I passed through one of the tunnels in the mountain, I got out of my car to take a picture. I didn't think about the wind being a factor until a gust came and slammed my door into the back of my head. The corner of the door hit me so hard I lost my balance and stumbled against the car. I had to take a second to figure out if I had been knocked out. I wasn't sure how bad I had been hit.

I was nervous to check the back of my head for blood. If there was blood, how was I supposed to get to the hospital? If I had been knocked out at all, how was I supposed to drive any further? Too many bad scenarios were going through my head, and I was relieved to know none of them would happen, since I wasn't bleeding. I hopped back in my car and continued on to Mt. Rushmore.

I stopped at a few more places along the way to take pictures. As the morning wore on, the fog started to lift, and the sun started to shine. By the time I got to Mount Rushmore, the sky was a piercing blue with very few clouds. I could not have asked for better weather.

The lines to park at Mount Rushmore were shorter than I anticipated. I was able to get through the front gate and park within a matter of 10 minutes. It may have helped that I was visiting at the

MY LIFE IN THE 50 STATES

beginning of fall. I grabbed my purse, locked the door to my car and made my way up the stairs of the parking garage.

I made my way up to the front of the visitor's center where I could see the Avenue of Flags. Through the flags waving in the wind, I caught my first glimpse of the Presidents etched in the side of the mountain. I decided to find the Arkansas and Texas flags before I really searched for the perfect view.

When you have seen a monument such as Mount Rushmore countless times in books, on the Internet and on television, it is almost surreal to see it in person. You think you can grasp the size and magnitude of the sculpture, but it is something different in person. Maybe it was the perfect weather and the perfect blue sky as its backdrop. I'm not sure. What I do know is that it was simply magnificent.

Everyone there was taking their own pictures; I didn't want to ask anyone to take mine. I did what I had been doing the entire trip and set my phone on an automatic timer, propped it up against my purse and ran to get in front. This time, I tripped on the bleacher and almost ate the concrete. Good thing I caught my balance in time, not only to prevent some broken teeth, but also to get in front of the camera for the perfect photo.

After my picture adventure, I just sat and stared at the mountain for about ten minutes. I kept thinking of all the men that worked on that, how long it took them, and how much they risked by being up there. I honestly cannot put into words how it felt to see Mount Rushmore in person. All I can tell you is to go see it for yourself.

TENNESSEE
December 2015

IN 2011, I RAN MY first half marathon with my friend, Dawn Stuckey. We decided to attack the Big D Half Marathon in Dallas. Both of us had a dream of completing a full marathon at some point in our lives.

Later that summer is when I found out I had a ruptured disc in my back. After exploring several alternative therapies, surgery was my last option. In April 2012, I had surgery on my back to help alleviate the pain and numbness it was causing. I was devastated because this meant running was going to be questionable after the surgery.

In July of 2015, shortly before I moved back to Arkansas, I attended a boot camp workshop for Juice Plus+® in San Antonio. It was there that I found out our amazing company was the title sponsor of the St. Jude's Marathon in Memphis, Tennessee, which is held the first weekend in December every year. I told my friend, AJ, that I would love to run the half-marathon course and that she should do it with me. AJ likes to run, but for her, the half marathon was pushing the distance.

Immediately after the conference was over, I told Ali of my

TENNESSEE

idea. To her knowledge, the registration was closed, but she was still going to ask. Never hurts to ask, right? Good thing she did, because they opened it back up, just for us! Ali, AJ and I planned to run the race in December.

Training for this was going to be interesting for me. I knew it would have to be a variety of things in order to train my lungs properly. I was not going to be able to train like most people and run a certain amount each day. I was able to find a trainer who designed a cross training program for me that would help me gear up to run the 13.1 miles.

The route we would take in Memphis was a forgiving one. Surprisingly, the streets of Memphis have little to no incline. The course ran through downtown Memphis, a stroll down Beale and the most important stretch, through the campus of St. Jude's. All of the money raised during the full, half and kids marathons was benefiting all of the children of St. Jude's Hospital. Those who were healthy enough on race day would come outside and cheer on a bunch of strangers who were helping raise money for their treatments against that deadly "C" word—cancer. When I first heard we would be running through campus, I was nothing short of excited. To see these children and their families would give anyone perspective on their own current situation, no matter what it was.

I did my best to prepare for this race. I never ran more than half a mile at one time. Some people may have thought this was not good training for a half marathon, but I felt it was the best I could do in order to stay healthy going into the race. My game plan going into the race was to run for 10 minutes and walk for two minutes for the entire race.

The Thursday before the race, Ali and AJ drove from Lawrence,

MY LIFE IN THE 50 STATES

Kansas, and stayed at my house in Fayetteville. The next morning, with my car packed with our race snacks, we drove to Memphis to meet everyone else. Since Juice Plus+® was the title sponsor for the race, there were many distributors running this race. Another friend of ours, Joy Kelly, would be running the race, as well as one of Ali's friends, Heidi Phillips.

After checking into the hotel, we had to check-in for the race and explore the vendors that were set up for the race. My nerves were starting to kick in, but I didn't want to admit it to anyone. I was extremely nervous. What if I couldn't finish? What if the pain in my back was just too much? What if I was the last person on the course? Too much doubt crept into my head, so I did what I was used to and just did my best to not even think about running. If someone brought up the race, I either left the conversation or changed the topic.

We had dinner at a local restaurant with Ali's brother-in-law, Brett, who had been living in Memphis for quite some time. Local spots are more of my favorite when traveling. I always want to experience something that is not in the town I live. We knew we could count on Brett to find us a good spot that would help us fuel up for the race the next day.

As we headed back to the hotel, I started feeling all the nerves rushing back to me. I was so anxious and excited, I did not know if I would be able to sleep! This was my first big physical challenge since I had my back surgery three and a half years prior. I started to believe I was going to finish, but I still wanted to challenge myself to come within 20 minutes of my previous time of 2:34:14. It wouldn't be easy, but I love a good challenge.

The morning of the race, we had to get up early enough to get some nutrition in our system without making us sick during the

155

TENNESSEE

race. I had a Chocolate Complete shake that our company makes, along with our capsules. The complete protein mix is amazing fuel because it is whole foods, nothing else. There are 10 different plants that make up the shake mix. The trio of capsules I took includes one fruit, one vegetable and one berry blend. These gave me a wide variety of 33 fruits, vegetables and berries with my normal dose, which is two of each. Since this was an important day, and I needed to fuel my body properly, I took triple the amount. Since these capsules are nothing but whole foods, I could take as many as I wanted because there is no risk of overdosing like there is with supplements.

After fueling up, we headed down to the baseball stadium to get ready for the race. Since it was early December, the weather was a bit chilly. Running would be a good thing to keep me warm. Being that we were running as a part of the Juice Plus+® family, we were allowed access to the suite in the baseball stadium.

I won't lie. Having this type of luxury was amazing on a chilly December morning. I saw the thousands of other runners who were freezing outside. This was also special because many of the top executives in our company were here, and Ali and Joy were able to introduce us to everyone. Our president, Jay Martin, and his wife were also participating in the race. He and his wife have participated in more than 14 of these races. Oh, and he was 70 years old at the time of this race.

All of the small talk and pre-race picture taking was able to keep my mind off my nerves, until someone said it was time to go. Here comes the adrenaline! As we headed downstairs and to the start, all I kept telling myself was 10 minutes at a time. That's all I had to do. Of course, I had to do almost three hours worth of 10 minutes at a time, but that was the goal. The closer we got to the start, the more I wanted it to hurry up and start.

156

MY LIFE IN THE 50 STATES

Big races, such as this one, have the start sectioned off for the different designated paces. Faster runners closer to the start and slower ones like me were further back. Ali headed towards the front, AJ was in the middle and I headed towards the back. As the race started, my time group slowly started to creep up and I was just ready to go. I am sure I had just as much adrenaline as I did blood flowing through my body at that point.

Once we crossed the start line, I was so excited! And then I quickly thought, *Am I really doing another half marathon?? 13.1 miles of running and walking?* Yes, indeed, I was. The first 10 minutes went by so fast and my body felt so good that I decided to run for 20 minutes and walk two minutes. After those 20 minutes, I decided I could run another 10. My body seemed as if it were ok, and I was in good enough shape to handle it. So then I ran for 30 and walked for five. I should have stuck to my original plan.

Between miles four and five, the route takes the runners through the campus of St. Jude's. As I mentioned before, any of the healthy patients would come outside to cheer on the runners with their homemade signs and noisemakers. I braced myself for this. The street was lined with so many of the nurses, patients and family members; it gave me an instant boost of energy. Those that were not well enough to come outside filled the windows of the buildings with more signs and smiles. These young people were the entire reason I was running—because I was able to. They were not, so I would run for them. They were so brave to be battling what they do every single day. I felt that my little back pain was nothing compared to what they were going through. I made sure that I ran the entire way through this campus, just for those patients.

After we left the campus, I noticed a difference in my legs. They started to get heavier and my muscles got tighter. Around

157

TENNESSEE

the 7.5-mile mark, I felt a pop in my hamstring. It wasn't a large pop, but it was enough that I was worried for the remaining 5.5 miles. I was so upset with myself that I didn't follow my original plan of running 10 minutes and walking two. I had a feeling that if I had, I wouldn't have had that pain. I struggled getting to the end, but I was confident I could do it.

When I saw the last mile marker, the adrenaline came rushing back to me. I found another gear. I wanted to finish strong. I picked up my pace as much as I could without burning out. The closer I got to the stadium, the more people were lined on the streets and the cheers got louder and louder. My pace picked up and I was giving it my all. I went all out, used every last bit of my energy and sprinted as hard as I could through the finish line. I didn't have my time on my watch. Somehow during the race I paused it. I walked around trying to cool down as best I could.

AJ called me and said she and Ali were up in the suite and to take my time. I wanted to find out my time. I just knew it wasn't as good as I wanted it to be, but I had to know. I went to the area where they printed off a sticker that had your time, what place you came in for your age group and the overall place. For females ages 35–39, I was in the middle of the pack, 519 out of 850. For all females it was about the same, 2,901 out of 4,384. Overall, I was 4,767 out of 7,702. The best part was my time at 2:41:14 with a pace of a 12:19 mile. This means I was exactly six minutes slower than my first half-marathon race. I realized I could have easily beaten my old time! When I first realized this, I was mad at myself. I quickly changed my thinking because that meant after all I had been through, I was still able to run an amazing race for an amazing cause. It wasn't about me. It was about raising money for those families and children who were unable to run. When you put that in perspective, I was a winner no matter what my time was.

TEXAS
February 2014

AT THE END OF February 2014, the race for the Southland Conference championship was getting heated. I was in my fourth year at Stephen F. Austin. Our last four games were crucial. We played on the road at Southeastern Louisiana and New Orleans and then came home to play Oral Roberts and Central Arkansas the following weekend. The Louisiana road trip coincided with the girls' basketball state tournament in Texas.

In my entire coaching career, I had never missed a game, but because Brandon was so confident in our chances of winning on the road, he decided it would be more beneficial for me to be at the state tournament.

When he first told me this, I was slightly upset, only because I do not like to miss games. Then when I realized it gave me the opportunity to go to San Antonio and see my grandmother, who had been in the hospital, I felt blessed to be able to go see her. My grandmother, Charlotte Nichols, was getting much older and her health was starting to decline. She had already fought colon cancer and had been in the nursing home for a few years. Add that to the fact she had already lived an amazing 94 years.

TEXAS

When I was younger, I spent some time in the hospital myself and volunteered in a nursing home. Now I have anxiety any time I set foot in either a hospital or nursing home. I am not sure why, but every time I get sweaty, my heart starts racing and I have trouble breathing. It isn't a full-blown panic attack, so I am able to hide it pretty easily. That feeling hit me hard the day I went to see my grandmother.

My schedule worked out perfectly to where I was able to go to the state tournament games, head south to San Antonio to see her and then back to Nacogdoches. After watching the last game I needed to see, I went to San Antonio. I was anxious the entire two-hour drive. I did not know what kind of shape I would see my grandmother in. She was a stubborn and ornery lady and I loved her with all my heart. I turned down the street the hospital was on and my heart started to race. When I pulled into the parking lot, my breaths shortened. I was getting nervous to see her. When I finally found a parking spot, I gave myself a bit of a pep talk, and went up to her room.

I found the room and was thankful to see my grandmother sitting up in the bed watching TV. My uncle Neil was with her. He and my mom split their time with her at the hospital. She looked tired, but was excited to see me. I had barely gotten a hug and a hello before the nurse came in to give her a quick bath. My uncle and I went to the waiting room while they did this.

When we got back to her room, I could tell she was pretty exhausted. Her appetite was not like it used to be, which caused her energy to be really low. We chatted for a little bit. She asked how our team was doing. She was very shocked that I wasn't in Louisiana with the team. I explained our situation to win the conference.

Since we had won both games that weekend, we needed to win our final two at home and Central Arkansas needed to lose both

MY LIFE IN THE 50 STATES

games on the road against Northwestern State and us. It was not going to be easy. We had lost to both ORU and UCA on the road earlier in the season, 64–55 and 65–42, respectively. Those games were our first since losing our starting point guard, Britney Matthew, to an ACL injury. Nonetheless, she was very excited to hear we had a shot.

Grandma was getting very tired, nodding off every few minutes. I had a five-hour drive back to Nacogdoches. I decided to let her rest and get on the road. She apologized each time she fell asleep and woke up. I told her there was no need to worry. I was just happy to sit there. She nodded off again, and I told my uncle I was getting on the road to head back. I gave him a hug, and as I started to walk out the door, I heard my grandmother call my name.

I turned around. "Yes ma'am?" I said.

"You tell those girls I said to go win it all."

I smiled and said, "Yes ma'am. I will tell them. Love you."

Those were the last words she said to me. Early Tuesday morning I got a phone call from my mom telling me she had passed away in her sleep.

I didn't know what to do. I was slightly numb, but somehow managed to fall back asleep after crying for I don't know how long. I sent a text to my head coach that she had died, and he said I could take whatever time I needed to and not to worry about coming in. I talked to my mom that morning to see what they were thinking about for her funeral. I hated to ask. I couldn't believe I even thought to ask. It hurt my stomach to ask, but I didn't have to. My mom said she knew what this week meant and knew that my grandmother would want me to be there to win the championship with the girls. My grandmother was my biggest fan. She said she was doing her best to have the funeral on Friday, so I wouldn't have to miss either game.

TEXAS

I didn't tell any of our players what had happened. To this day, I don't know how many of them know. I came to practice that Tuesday and Wednesday because I couldn't just sit in my apartment and stare at the walls. My mom and aunt both assured me that I didn't need to come home because realistically there was nothing for me to do there. On Thursday, our team came out on fire and we thrashed Oral Roberts 72–52, and I left immediately after the game. I made it to Kenedy about 2:00 a.m.

The funeral was at noon on Friday, so I was able to get some sleep that morning. My grandmother was well-known in the community, and our little church was packed. It was great to see so many people there to honor her. My younger cousin was even able to fly in from Ecuador. It was actually the first time ever that all nine of us grandchildren were together. It was soul-soothing to be around all the family and friends of my grandmother. I thought I was going to drive back Friday night, but I was mentally, physically and emotionally exhausted. I texted Brandon to let him know I would not be back in time for our shootaround on Saturday, but I would be there in time for the game.

I know many would think it was crazy that I would leave my family so soon after the funeral. But if you knew my grandmother, you would know that being at the game is exactly where she would have wanted me to be.

It was hard driving back to Nacogdoches on Saturday morning, and I started to tear up several times. I kept reminding myself of the goal for the day—beat UCA for the outright conference title. And that is what we did. We beat UCA 61–41, and cut down the nets at home that night. We did just as my grandmother had told me to do. The girls went and won it all.

162

UTAH
2008, 2009, and 2010

THE ONLY TIME I TRAVELED here was for basketball. Utah State was in our conference when I coached at San Jose State. This meant once a year, for the three years I coached, I flew into Salt Lake City with the team and we made the hour and a half drive to Logan. The drive was very scenic with the mountains to the east and the Great Salt Lake to our left.

Each time we played at Utah State, we made sure to stop in at Wingers. Wingers had the absolute best wings I have ever tasted. I wouldn't call myself a connoisseur of wings, but I have traveled and tried enough to vouch for these. I'm not sure what it is, but these wings are the best. They are so good that I would always look to see if there was a Wingers in other cities we traveled to.

Once, I had the bus driver take me to the restaurant and order some for after a game. Like others, Utah is a state I would like to visit again in the summer and explore everything the state has to offer. I wish I had a better story to tell you of this state, but maybe that is for next time.

VERMONT
August 2016

HIKING AND EXPLORING A NEW place has become a favorite pastime of mine. When I started planning my road trip through New England, I wanted to find a trail to hike, so I could enjoy some of the beauty of the New England nature. As I was searching for places to visit, I came across a trail called Texas Falls, and I immediately knew that is where I needed to go.

My first night in Vermont, I stayed in White River Junction. Texas Falls was about an hour from Hartford and only slightly off my route to Burlington, which is where I planned to stay for the next night. The drive to Texas Falls was stunning. The highway was lined on both sides with tall vibrant trees. I have always enjoyed a relaxing road trip. The clear sunny sky and all that green vegetation sure helped it to be just that.

To be honest, I am always nervous about hiking alone in an unfamiliar territory. I am more worried about wildlife than I am people. I didn't research any type of safety tips regarding encountering any wildlife, which raised my anxiety level more than normal. I also believe that if I let the anxiety take over, then I would never get to see anything. I would miss out on too many

VERMONT

experiences and opportunities. That's why I believe that if it is my time to go, it's my time to go (even if I get mauled by a bear).

I found my way to the parking lot of the park and found the trailhead for Texas Falls. The forest was breezy and shaded from the August sun. Even though there were several signs posted not to swim in the creek, several teenagers were doing so. My first thought was, *Why aren't they in school?* But then I remembered it was still August, and they may still be out of school for the summer.

The loop around Texas Falls is only a mile and rated as an easy hike. I took in the scenery, listened to the streaming water and spent time searching for the best photo opportunities I could, and all of that only took me about 30 minutes to complete. As I walked back to the car, I couldn't help but remember how lucky I was to be able to visit somewhere off the beaten path in the state of Vermont.

I headed north to Burlington for the rest of the day. Since I had some extra time before dinner, I decided to get dressed up for dinner. I planned to be in leggings and t-shirts for the entire trip, but getting dolled up for dinner one evening seemed like a good idea. I showered, curled my hair, did my makeup and was headed out the door to dinner in downtown Burlington. I opened the door to the outside of the hotel and had to sprint to my car because a thunderstorm had rolled in. I didn't hear any of that rain while I was getting ready. I sprinted to the car and decided it just added another laugh to my life.

I ventured downtown to eat dinner at a local restaurant. When eating out alone, I usually opt to sit in the bar. This allows me to engage in some conversation with the bartender and some of the other people at the bar. Plus, the bar area has televisions and I

166

MY LIFE IN THE 50 STATES

can be entertained while I eat. I also have learned not to drink much alcohol, if any at all, while dining alone because of what happened in Florida.

I happened to sit down next to two gentlemen who were in town on business. Both worked for USA Hockey, or at least that is what they told me. The only hockey experience I have ever had is when I was in junior college at Odessa College working as a student trainer. The student trainers were on a rotation to help with our local minor league hockey team. A hockey team in west Texas was comical in itself.

In our conversation, I mentioned why I was in town. I revealed to them what states I had left at the time, and both said I needed to go to Michigan in the winter when they have a hockey tournament outdoors on the frozen lake. I looked at them like they had three heads each. These strangers did not understand I do not like the cold. However, the more and more they told me about this tournament, I thought it would be an interesting event to attend, with multiple layers and heavy-duty jackets. After dinner, I headed back to my hotel to rest up for another long drive the next day.

The next day I went to the shore of Lake Champlain to take some pictures. Had I more time, I would have taken a dinner cruise on the lake. It was quite a windy and chilly morning. I was shocked at how cold it was in the middle of August. Once I reminded myself how far north I was, it all made a little more sense. I took a stroll along the shore of the lake through the park. Another thing about being by myself on these travels is that sometimes I find myself speeding through my sightseeing, which isn't always a good thing.

I had more time to kill before lunch, so I went walking around

VERMONT

downtown. Church Street is one of the main streets running through the downtown area. The street is made of red brick and there is a large portion of the street that is set aside as a walking marketplace rather than driving. I came upon a University of Vermont bookstore. This was the perfect place for me to grab a keychain. Finally, it was time for some lunch! I wanted lunch as soon as possible because I was headed to tour Ben & Jerry's factory shop.

In Texas, we have the popular Blue Bell ice cream, which is made in Brenham, Texas. I believe Blue Bell is the best single flavor ice cream, and Ben & Jerry's is the best novelty ice cream. I did not know what to expect when I arrived at the creamery. I definitely didn't expect a two-hour wait to take the tour. I decided to skip the tour, grab some ice cream and take a walk around the grounds. Ben & Jerry's now has dairy-free ice cream, and the *PB & Cookies* flavor is simply amazing! I took a walk around the picnic tables that were set up and headed over to the Flavor Graveyard. This is where all of the flavors that are discontinued, such as *This is Nuts, Turtle Soup* and *Schweddy Balls*, are buried. After reading the ingredients to some of them, I understand why they are buried. Some just need a name change.

There are other places I would love to hike and explore in Vermont that I didn't get the chance to. However, my time was limited, and I had to hop in the car and head to Maine.

VIRGINIA
Multiple and Random

THIS IS A STATE THAT I have driven across or visited on a short-term basis, but never stopped to do anything in. I drove across the state when I was in college driving from Arkansas to Washington, D.C., to spend Christmas with my parents.

I had to drive back across the very northern part to avoid a massive snowstorm in Tennessee. I was there shortly overnight when I stayed for Gigi's wedding. That was part of the story in Maryland.

I also went to Malcom's (Gigi's brother) wedding in southern Virginia. I drove up from my parents' home in Rural Hall, North Carolina, for the ceremony. It is weird, but nothing major has happened in this state for me, although I have traveled across it several times.

WASHINGTON
September 2011

I had been working at SFA for a year when Megan went to work at the University of Washington (UW) in her hometown of Seattle. Angela stayed in San Jose and was working for a nonprofit. We decided it was time that we have a Charlie's Angels reunion in Seattle for Labor Day weekend. It was risky taking a trip once school had started because of the uncertainty of how Labor Day weekend can go in college athletics. Angela and I knew we could occupy ourselves if duties called for Megan to have to work.

Since the flight there is so long, I decided to fly up on Thursday evening. Megan picked me up from the airport and we headed to her parents' house in Bellevue. My body was on Central Standard Time, and even as excited as I was to see Megan, I needed sleep. I crawled into bed, started to dose off and my phone rang. It was one of my best friends, Kenya Landers. It isn't normal for her to call me, and especially to call so late; she is a text kind of girl. When I answered, she was whispering. I asked if everything was ok, and she said she was in the emergency room because her stomach was hurting so bad. She didn't know if it was acid reflux

WASHINGTON

or what. My first thought was, *Are you pregnant?* So I asked her. Kenya said no because she had just taken a pregnancy test *TWO* days before at the doctor's office. To rule it out again, they gave her another pregnancy test and it came back positive. She already had a daughter, Michaela, but wasn't expecting to have baby #2 so soon. I was falling asleep on the phone, so she said she would text me with the results. I woke up to a text saying it was positive. Baby Landers #2 was on the way!

The next morning Megan and I packed up our bags and headed to the airport to pick up Angela. Megan's brother lived closer to where we wanted to be for the weekend, so he offered his house to us since he and his family would not be there for the weekend. After we came back from picking up Angela, we headed to a nail salon near where Megan's mom, Sandy, works. She had picked up gift certificates for us to get a manicure or pedicure. We got caught up over nails and mimosas, and then headed over to eat lunch. Megan took us on a tour of the basketball facilities at Washington. The University is on a quarter system, so students were not on campus just yet. This is what made it easier for Megan to hang out with us for the weekend.

When we arrived at Megan's brother's house, she had a present for Angela and me. Leave it to Megan to think of something for us to have for the weekend. She got each of us a University of Washington t-shirt to wear to the football game the next day. She also got us field passes for the pregame warm-up. It is great to have friends in the college athletic world.

Saturday morning, we went shopping for necessities to tailgate. Megan was technically working on Saturday because they had a prospective student-athlete on an unofficial visit for the day. We grabbed some snacks and headed to the football stadium.

MY LIFE IN THE 50 STATES

It was the first game of the year, and we didn't want to spend it driving around trying to find the parking lot where we were supposed to park.

Growing up in Bellevue, Megan played with several players who continued their playing career at UW. It was a reunion of sorts when she had a few of those former teammates and friends come by and meet us before we headed into the game. If you ever have the chance to get field passes to a football game, do it! I didn't think it would be that big of a deal, but it ended up being an exciting experience. Starting with the energy that you feel on the field from the players, to the band and the music being played, it is a different type of energy.

The Huskies were playing Eastern Washington, and on paper it should have been an easy game. Eastern Washington stayed in the game all the way until the end, but the Huskies pulled out the first win of the season 30–27. We were set to celebrate that evening with a fun night out.

We loaded up and headed back to the house to get dressed and head out for the night. After a long day at the football game and a soothing hot shower, all three of us could have easily called it a night. We got dressed to motivate us to go, but it was a slow motivation. We seemed to find ways of stalling our departure. Megan started sharing pictures. I was looking for something to eat. I think Angela was just going to go with the flow, whether we went out or stayed at home in our pajamas. We finally got a push to make it out the door. It was a valiant effort that lasted about an hour and a half. We had a drink, maybe two, at the first bar we went to, found a 24-hour diner to get something to eat and headed home. Not every night out has to be a drunken night to be memorable.

WASHINGTON

The next day, Megan planned for us to picnic at one of her favorite locations. Alki Beach is along the Puget Sound and looks back along the city skyline. It was a beautiful day and perfect for a picnic. We loaded up the car with food, a few choice adult beverages, and made our way to the park. Being that close to the water was very windy. We had to weight everything down with a bottle or drink or foot. At some point the wind picked up enough that it looked as if we were playing twister trying to keep everything down.

One of our favorite things to do is take jumping pictures, where we try to time the shot just right as we are jumping in the air. We each took an individual shot and then tried a group shot. This time around would prove to be difficult because Angela recently had knee surgery, in addition to using a timer on the camera and having it catching all three of us jumping at the right moment. Several great outtakes later, we nailed our shot.

Since we only had the afternoon remaining in Seattle, we made our way downtown to look into taking a Duck Tour around the city. The duck boats are the boats that travel on land and water. This was going to be our best bet for all three of us to enjoy seeing everything in Seattle.

Before we got out of the car, I decided to chug the remainder of the drink I had and then make a roadie for the tour. A roadie is a drink to take with you on the road. This may or may not have been the smartest decision, especially for someone like me who has to pee every 10 minutes. But hey, what's a little adventure, right?

We purchased our tickets for the next available tour. We had some time to kill, so we walked over to the Space Needle. Angela and I were good with not going up to the top. We browsed the

174

MY LIFE IN THE 50 STATES

visitor's center and gift shop while sipping on our drinks. Of course, I bought my keychain. After killing time, we found our way back to the duck boat tour and realized we were going to enjoy this tour a lot more than most of the people on the boat. It was not my intention to get tipsy before I hopped on, but that is what happened.

The tour took us past the original Starbucks, Pike Place Market and along the shore of the Puget Sound where *Sleepless in Seattle* was filmed.

About halfway through the tour, I was beginning to realize exactly how bad an idea drinking that much prior to the tour was. And then we reached the part where the boat entered the water. Being in rough choppy water was a strain on my bladder. It felt like someone was hitting my bladder from all sides. I did not enjoy the last 15 minutes of the boat tour. As soon as the boat got to our drop off, I sprinted to the bathroom. Never felt so much relief in my life!

That weekend was full of laughs and love from my angels. We went through a lot together at San Jose State and created a special bond. No matter where we are in life, those two will always be able to make me smile, laugh and fill my heart with a special love.

175

WEST VIRGINIA
May 2017

ONE OF THE ANGELS IS getting married! As I mentioned before, Megan, Angela and I were nicknamed Charlie's Angels when we worked together at San Jose State. It has finally come time for one of the angels to get married! Megan was marrying long-time boyfriend, Joe Westerfer. Coming into this weekend, we knew it would be epic, every little detail accounted for, and every day scheduled down to the minute because that's what Megan does.

Angela and I were set to fly into Pittsburgh, pick up a few of the groomsmen and head to Wheeling, West Virginia. Megan's grandparents lived here, and she spent many summers visiting from her home state of Washington. The wedding was being held at Oglebay Resort. If you have ever seen the original *Dirty Dancing* movie, that is exactly what this place reminded us all of—acres of golf courses, a variety of cottages and rooms, swimming pools and restaurants. It is not what I had pictured West Virginia to look like. I can honestly say I had no idea what to expect, but Wheeling is beautiful.

I arrived earlier than everyone else, so I spent some time

WEST VIRGINIA

eating lunch and doing some random shopping before I picked up Angela, along with Mike Neighbors and Todd Schaefer, the two groomsmen. Once Neighbors packed the car like a game of Tetris, we made the short one-hour drive to Wheeling. Wheeling is in the skinny part of the state of West Virginia, on the border of Pennsylvania and Ohio. The highway follows the Ohio River and is right across from Steubenville, Ohio. If you are a sports fan, particularly football, you may have heard of Steubenville. I won't go into details here because there is plenty about it that you can read online.

We arrived at the resort, checked in and went to the bar. It's a wedding and a weekend; that is what you do. Soon, Megan, Joe and several other guests showed up, and the entertainment began. It also happened to be Joe's 50th birthday, so there was a lot to celebrate. The drinking and socializing continued until about 2:00 a.m., when Angela and I finally decided it was time for us to go to bed. We had a very full day scheduled on Friday.

On Friday morning, all of the bridesmaids headed over to a local day spa where we had appointments to get manicures and pedicures. I was one of the first people in the chair for my toes and I opted out of getting a manicure. I noticed a sign that the spa also had massage services. I asked a few questions regarding rates, and then asked Angela if she thought it was ok if went and got a massage while everyone else got their manicures. She didn't think it would be rude, especially since my back had been causing me problems the week leading up to the wedding. I went ahead and asked Megan how she felt about it and she was all for it. It made me feel better that she was ok with it.

I did not realize this until I was sitting in the room waiting for the massage therapist to walk in, that the spa had actually called

178

MY LIFE IN THE 50 STATES

her in early for me. I was glad I made this decision. I did not want to be at the dinner rehearsal and wedding in heels all weekend and not be able to walk the next week.

After the spa, all of us headed back to the hotel to have a late lunch in Sandy's suite (Megan's mother). Megan was a detailed planner and organizer. One thing Megan did not plan on was a surprise her mother and matron of honor, Jackie, had in store for her.

Jackie was one of Megan's college teammates and dearest friends. Unexpectedly, Jackie and her husband became pregnant and the due date was within weeks of Megan's wedding. She did her best to arrange to still be a part of the wedding, but it just wasn't going to work out. Sandy still wanted Jackie to be a part of the wedding somehow and came up with a great idea to surprise Megan. Jackie took a photo in her matron of honor dress and Sandy had a life-size standup of the picture made for Megan.

When Megan arrived at the luncheon, Angela and I were in the bedroom portion of the suite with the life-size Jackie. Sandy gave Megan an excuse as to why she needed to go into the bedroom. When she first opened the sliding door, she was a bit surprised to see Angela crouching on the floor holding her phone up to record. Then she turned her head to see the life-size image of Jackie. She hugged her as if it were really Jackie. A tear or two may have been shed.

During the lunch, Megan gave us our bridesmaids' gifts, which included a robe to wear the following day while we were having our makeup done, and jewelry for the day of the wedding. This is where all of the detailed planning came into play. She hand-picked our jewelry from her and Joe's jeweler in Philadelphia.

The rehearsal dinner was scheduled for this same evening,

179

WEST VIRGINIA

so after the luncheon, all of the girls went their separate ways to relax a bit and get ready for the dinner. When it was time, we all made our way to the outdoor amphitheater where the ceremony would take place. West Virginia in May at 5:00 p.m. is quite hot, and the sun was setting directly on us. We wanted to make this as quickly as possible, so we could get out of the sun and enjoy the food! To our surprise, all of the groomsmen showed up on time, and we only had to practice three times. Most of us were coaches, former coaches or former athletes. We are all very coachable.

Dinner was very special, as several of Megan and Joe's family spoke about the excitement they had for the other to be joining the family, as well as the love they had for them. Her nephew, Henry, had the best story about Joe taking him to play pool at the bar at Megan's sister's wedding. That is when he knew Joe was a keeper. Wedding day, or "game day" as we referred to it, was starting at 8:00 a.m. the next day, so we kept our night short. We knew we wanted to have all of our energy for the following day and night.

It's finally game day! Bright and early Saturday morning, the bridesmaids loaded up in both my rental car and Megan's SUV and headed to the salon to get our hair and makeup done. Again, Megan thought of everything and had mimosas, fruit and pastries for us at the salon. By noon, we were all dolled up and headed back to the hotel to have lunch in Sandy's suite. All seven bridesmaids got dressed in the suite and waited. By the time we got dressed, we had about two hours until the trolley picked us up to take pictures with the rest of the bridal party. After several photo shoots and a near disastrous fall out of the trolley by yours truly, it was game time!

The ceremony went off without a hitch! And Joe and Megan were hitched! It was time to celebrate! We had a cocktail hour in

MY LIFE IN THE 50 STATES

a garden area before the reception started. It was great to meet so many of Megan's friends that we had heard about for so many years. The reception was an all-out party and ended perfectly when Joe and one of his friends from Philly, Marty, recreated "the jump" that Patrick Swayze and Jennifer Grey did in the movie *Dirty Dancing*. To give you a better idea of how comical and impressive this was, Joe is 6'5" and weighs 260 pounds, and Marty is 6'1" and weighs 215 pounds.

The next day, Megan's family had a barbecue for everyone and we took that day to recover. My flight wasn't until Monday, as was Angela and Todd's. Recovering before our flight home was needed. We all had an amazing time in West Virginia, thanks to our girl, Megan.

WISCONSIN
September 2017

DURING MY FOUR-STATE ROAD TRIP, Wisconsin was first on deck. When I was putting my trip together, I looked up sports schedules first. It was September, which meant great football weather. I again went to my greatest resource, Facebook, to see if anyone had any connections with tickets to a Wisconsin football game. I was quickly reminded that the nutritionist at Arkansas, Karla Horsfall, had just moved from Wisconsin. I gave Karla a call and she was able to help me out with a ticket.

Traveling alone can be expensive if you stay in hotels. Luckily for me, Airbnb has become more and more popular. I was expecting anything close to the stadium to be expensive over a football weekend, but somehow managed to find a great room about a mile from the stadium and at an amazing price of $53 a night. Parking around a football stadium can be a nightmare, so walking the short walk was perfect for me, especially since the weather was supposed to be perfect football weather.

The morning of the football game was sunny with a clear blue sky, but it was 32 degrees. I panicked because I forgot to bring any type of jacket. Target to the rescue. I was at the store in time for

WISCONSIN

it to open and found a sweater I could wear. I had to rush back home because it was an early kick off that Saturday. I wanted to be there to feel the energy of that stadium. I had watched several Wisconsin games on television before and had heard it was a great place to watch games.

Lucky for me, it got warmer as the day went on. I started my walk to the stadium slightly worried that I would be cold. As soon as my blood started flowing and the sun started shining brighter, I got warmer. Almost too warm.

The neighborhood was an older one and the homes were not the same type of homes I am used to. Down in the south, most homes have two car garages with good-sized yards, even the older homes. These homes had single car garages that were basically underneath the house. The homes were taller than they were wide, and you could pretty much see into your neighbor's kitchen from your own kitchen. Although the homes were different and beautiful, I like my spacious home and privacy.

I trusted my GPS to get me to the stadium. I was paranoid that I was walking the wrong way until I saw more people in red and white going the same direction I was going. Paid parking signs started showing up. Music started to get louder from people tailgating. My nerves settled, knowing I was at least in the general vicinity. And then I saw it—the end zone of Camp Randall Stadium. This stadium has been the Wisconsin football stadium since 1917. Over the years there have been renovations, but the unique part about it is the original field house is still a part of the stadium. Newer, modern facilities were built on the side, but the University kept the field house that had been built in 1930.

I found my way to the will-call office to pick up my ticket. When I ask someone for a free ticket, I do not care where the

184

MY LIFE IN THE 50 STATES

seats are. They are FREE! I am just happy to be there. The sound of the band and rustling crowd started to give me chills. I am a college sports fan. I love the atmosphere it creates. I love the rush of adrenaline a good play gives you.

I am one of those people who will watch a game and try to dissect and understand the game plan from a coach's point of view and not just cheer for the home team because it is the home team. I think about everything involved with being a part of a college team; from the hours they put into the practice, to the injury situation for the week and how the student-athletes were functioning mentally.

As I stepped through the tunnel leading into the stadium, all I saw was a sea of red. I paused for a few seconds to take in the view of the clear skies, sun shining down on the crowd and the sound of the music playing over the stadium speakers. I made my way to my seat. The view was amazing! Being higher up at a football game is a good thing. Since the field is so large, you can see much more if you are higher as opposed to lower. My seat was on the 20-yard line and midway up the stadium, which in my mind, was perfect!

The first half of the game was intense. Northwestern was the underdog in this game, but went into halftime up 10–7. The Badgers came out of halftime on fire, going ahead 21–10. It was then time for one of the best traditions in college football. In between the third and fourth quarters, the entire stadium, including the old folks, jumped to the song *Jump Around* by House of Pain. It is one of those traditions that you would normally feel awkward doing, but when 80,000 other people are doing it, you don't feel as awkward. (Similar to how I felt the first time I Called the Hogs at an Arkansas Razorback football game.) This makes

185

WISCONSIN

the energy in the stadium electrifying. When I told my friends from Wisconsin I was going to the game, every single one of them said I needed to stay for that, no matter what the score was.

Midway through the fourth quarter, Wisconsin seemed to have put the game away, going up 31–10. I rarely leave a game early. I like to watch them all the way until the end, because you never know what might happen.

With 4:46 left in the game, Northwestern scored another touchdown to bring the game to 31–17. Two minutes later, they scored another to make it a one-possession game. Looking to tie the game with under a minute left, Northwestern made a critical error and Wisconsin was able to get a safety and put the game out of reach for Northwestern. Situations like these are exactly why it is good to stay to the end.

WYOMING
March 2013

WYOMING HAS A SCENIC LANDSCAPE. There's the open range and no skylines polluting the air. You can get lost in the never-ending scenery. The first time I visited the state was a quick drive, cutting through the southeastern part of the state on my way to Nebraska. I was recruiting a player, Destiny Bragman, who was leading the country in junior college for blocked shots. She was playing at the regional tournament at Western Nebraska Community College in Scottsbluff, Nebraska. Scottsbluff is not the easiest place to get to. I decided I would fly into Denver and make the short three-hour drive.

Being from south Texas, I am not a fan of cold weather. Have I said that already? I only saw snow twice before graduating high school, and one of those times we drove to see it. When I landed in Denver, my knees immediately felt the cold. Luckily, I was driving and not riding a horse to Nebraska, so I was going to be warm for the most part.

Back in 2012, I had back surgery, and now sitting down for more than an hour gets very uncomfortable. I have to get out and stretch as much as I can, without breaking up the trip too much.

WYOMING

My first stop was Cheyenne, Wyoming, at a gas station. Even though it was a beautiful sunny day, I could feel how cold it was outside just by touching the window. I did NOT want to get out of my car. I knew what would happen if I did. As soon as I opened the door, the wind slapped me in the face like I had talked about its mother. It was brutally cold. I made this the quickest stop possible. I ran inside the gas station to use the restroom, stretch a little bit and grab something to drink. I decided to run to the car this time, thinking it would be faster and maybe even not as cold, and boy was I wrong. The wind made it colder and my blood did not circulate fast enough to get warm. I couldn't get the car started fast enough to get the heat going.

Scottsbluff, Nebraska, wasn't much warmer, but again, I was going to be inside most of the day. After the game that evening, I headed back to Denver, since I had a morning flight. My stop happened in Cheyenne again, and this time it was at night. I had never in my 33 years of life (at that time) been in temperatures in the teens. It was 12 degrees when I got out to put gas in my car. My entire body hurt. It was then I realized that I didn't ever want to be in temperatures lower than my age.

The only other time I have been to Wyoming was during the crazy ass road trip my cousins and I took when moving my uncle down to Texas from Watson Lake, Yukon Territory. I slept through that drive, since it was in the middle of the night. There are several things I would love to see in Wyoming: the Grand Teton Mountains, Old Faithful and all of Yellowstone, just to name a few. Next time, it will be in the summer.

BONUS INFO

Arizona: Visiting Sedona with my dear friends, Sam, AJ and LA, for my birthday; Slide Rock Park; falling over the last hurdle in the regional track meet as a sophomore in high school; beating the University of Arizona on their home floor while coaching at SFA.

Arkansas: My name being engraved on the Walk of Graduates at the University of Arkansas; help tearing down the goal posts when Arkansas football beat Tennessee; rushing the court when men's basketball beat #2 Auburn; sledding down the hills on cafeteria trays on campus during snow storm.

California: San Diego Zoo, Warriors and Raiders games, NCAA Tournament host; my second tattoo; beating then #22 California on their home floor 68–66.

Colorado: Women's Final Four.

BONUS INFO

Florida: A Women's Final Four, Juice Plus+® Conference, Thanksgiving tournament that had me at Kinko's at 4:00 a.m., copying scouting reports and panhandle beach trips.

Georgia: Working camps at the University of Georgia is where I was first put in charge of an entire gym full of campers. It made me feel overwhelmed, but it gave me a sense of pride that I was good at my job that the staff felt comfortable putting me in charge of an entire gym.

Hawaii: Sneaking away at 6:30 a.m. with our sports information director to try and get into Pearl Harbor on the day we were flying back to San Jose; swimming with sharks on Oahu's North Shore.

Idaho: First time experiencing Wingers.

Illinois: The Navy Pier, the place I bought my first suit and first Coach purse (I named her Lily) and where I learned that young people really don't know how to read a map and are truly shocked when I can.

Kansas: Lots of basketball camps, Late Night in the Phog (google it, basketball fans) and seeing Destiny's Child and Nelly at an amphitheater.

Kentucky: Basketball is the only experience I have in this state. From the one mentioned previously, to another all-night drive to see Arkansas play Kentucky, to more recent basketball tournaments of me coaching a summer club team.

MY LIFE IN THE 50 STATES

Louisiana: Working basketball camps at Louisiana Tech and Louisiana State University.

North Carolina: First concert ever, Tina Turner; watching Wake Forest vs. Duke men's basketball; watching my best friend, Gigi (Miller) Johnson, compete at NCAA Outdoor National Track Championships.

Michigan: NCAA Men's basketball tournament 2018; Motown Records

Mississippi: Spending Thanksgiving with my aunt and uncle, and I slept 30 of the 48 hours I was there.

Missouri: Attending Yvonne's high school graduation (the youngest child of Coach A & Marcheita Anderson).

Nebraska: Stopping in Omaha to see Kylee Coulter, a former club player, as she was attending the University of Nebraska, Omaha.

Oklahoma: Losing to Tulsa University on New Year's Day.

Oregon: Recruiting at the Nike Tournament End of the Trail and getting free passes to the Nike Employee store at Nike Headquarters; almost getting thrown off a horse at a friend's ranch.

Pennsylvania: Spending the day in Pittsburgh after Megan's wedding and ALMOST getting another tattoo.

191

BONUS INFO

South Carolina: Taking a road trip from Arkansas to the NCAA Men's Basketball tournament in 2017.

Tennessee: Women's Final Four; first Juice Plus+® conference; road trip across the state driving from Arkansas to North Carolina for the summer and crashed into a road construction barrel (no workers were present and no one was harmed).

Texas: Beating the University of Arizona for a second straight year; capturing two conference championships on our home court at SFA; floating the Comal River; beach trips to Port Aransas; toilet papering the campus at Odessa College; driving my Ford Aspire on the sidewalks at Odessa College.

Washington: Discovering the Death by Chocolate Cake in Seattle after our Alaskan cruise.

During the time of my travels, it was not in my forethought to someday write a book detailing my "adventures" in each state. Once I decided to write about my journey, I realized that I couldn't remember the names of some of the places (restaurants, landmarks, stores, etc.) I visited. With the help of some of my traveling companions, I have been able to go back and fill in some of those missing details.

50 STATES GALLERY

MY LIFE IN THE 50 STATES

Alaska: Scott Greve (brother), Jessica Greve (sister-in-law), me on whale watching excursion.

50 STATES GALLERY

Alaska: Train ride in Skagway.

Alaska: Train ride in Skagway.

196

MY LIFE IN THE 50 STATES

Alaska: Me in front of glacier at Tracy Arm Fjord.

50 STATES GALLERY

Alaska: Me on the crab fishing boat *Aleutian Ballad*.

Hawaii: Me, Jessica (sister-in-law), Scott (brother) getting ready to head down on bikes from Haleakala.

MY LIFE IN THE 50 STATES

Hawaii: John (dad), Diane (mom), Aiden (nephew), Jessica (sister-in-law), Scott (brother), Riley (nephew), me.

Hawaii: Me, John (dad), Jessica (sister-in-law), Scott (brother), Aiden (nephew) after helicopter tour.

50 STATES GALLERY

Hawaii: Jessica (sister-in-law), Scott (brother), and I in helicopter.

Hawaii: Me at Diamond Head State Park.

MY LIFE IN THE 50 STATES

Maine: Where I
read my DNA results.

50 STATES GALLERY

Maine: Me at Maine state line.

Maine: Cape Elizabeth Lighthouse.

MY LIFE IN THE 50 STATES

Maryland: Gigi (Miller) Johnson and I at her wedding.

Massachusetts: Beach at Cape Cod.

50 STATES GALLERY

Minnesota: Me in front of Minnehaha Falls.

Missouri: Me crossing the stage at the Juice Plus+® Conference in St Louis.

204

MY LIFE IN THE 50 STATES

Montana: Justin Mayes, Keely (Mayes) Engel, Larry Kiesling, Jr., me at The Battle of the Little Bighorn.

Nebraska: TD Ameritrade Park, College World Series 2018, Arkansas vs Oregon State Game 1.

50 STATES GALLERY

Nevada: Tana (Pyle) Drennan and I at Toby Keith's.

MY LIFE IN THE 50 STATES

New York: Me in front of Madison Square Garden.

50 STATES GALLERY

New York: Me in front of
Rockefeller Center Christmas Tree.

MY LIFE IN THE 50 STATES

North Dakota: Me in front of the world's largest buffalo, Jamestown, ND.

Pennyslvania: Me at the Liberty Bell.

50 STATES GALLERY

South Dakota: Tunnel through Needles Highway
where car door hit me in my head
as I took this picture.

MY LIFE IN THE 50 STATES

South Dakota: Lake along Needles Highway.

50 STATES GALLERY

South Dakota: Mount Rushmore.

MY LIFE IN THE 50 STATES

South Dakota: Me at state line.

50 STATES GALLERY

Tennessee: St Jude's half marathon start, L to R AJ Majors, Joy Kelly, Ali Schneider, Heidi Phillips, me.

Tennessee: Before the St Jude's Half Marathon AJ Majors, me, Ali Schneider.

MY LIFE IN THE 50 STATES

Texas: Me and my grandmother, Charlotte Nichols, at her last Christmas.

50 STATES GALLERY

Texas: Kali "KK" Jerrell and Tierany Henderson SFA vs UCA (*Photo credit Hardy Meredith, Stephen F. Austin*).

Texas: Team after we clinched conference title vs UCA (*Photo credit Hardy Meredith, Stephen F. Austin*).

MY LIFE IN THE 50 STATES

Vermont: Me in front of
Texas Falls sign.

50 STATES GALLERY

Washington: Megan (Osmer) Westerfer, Angela Gonzaga, me, University of Washington football game.

MY LIFE IN THE 50 STATES

West Virginia: Megan (Osmer) Westerfer and me at her beautiful wedding.

50 STATES GALLERY

Wisconsin: Me at the state line.

Wisconsin: Camp Randall Stadium,
Wisconsin vs Northwestern.

CONTACT INFORMATION

If you would like to follow more of my journey, need information regarding health coaching or speaking engagements, please visit www.jodithegypsy.com.

If you would like more information regarding the products I used for my half marathon training, please visit www.jodigreve.juiceplus.com.

Follow me on:

- Jodi Greve
- @jodithegypsy
- @CoachJodi_
- Jodi Greve

Made in the USA
Columbia, SC
19 September 2019